SOLSTICE CELEBRATIONS

Also By

Amy Virginia Evans

Fantastically Fabulous February

SOLSTICE CELEBRATIONS

History, Crafts, Food

Amy Virginia Evans

Illustrations by Amy Virginia Evans

OPENAMUSE

OPENAMUSE

SOLSTICE CELEBRATIONS

Copyright © 2017 Amy Virginia Evans

Printed in the United States of America.

Illustrations by Amy Virginia Evans

ISBN 978-1522747741

For Michael.

With gratitude, for all of the seasons.

Hymn to the Sun

The people of Latium call you Sol

Because you alone are the crown of light

Held in honor after the Father.

They claim that your sacred head,

Brilliant with twelve rays,

Shines forth as many golden beams

As months of the year,

As sunlit hours of the day.

They say that you control four steeds with reins,

For you alone drive the chariot that nature furnishes.

Restraining the darkness,

You reveal the blue sky with your light,

So they call you Phoebus,

Foreteller of the future's secrets,

Or Lycaeus, because you break up the night's excesses.

The Nile worships you as Serapis,

Memphis adores you as Osiris,

Other cults revere you as Mithra, Dis, or Savage Typhon.

You are known as fair Attis

and the gentle boy of the curved ploy.

The parched Libyans pray to you as Ammon,

and Byblos, as Adon.

So the whole world calls upon you under different names.

Martianus Capella, Fourth Century CE
Translated by Florence Marie Berdes, C.S.J.

Contents

Sun Stands Still

Winter solstice marks the beginning of a season and an opportunity to contemplate the endless cycle of humankind's struggle to overcome darkness and decay. Solstice means "sun stands still" in Latin. In the Northern Hemisphere, this shortest day and longest night of the year occurs on December twenty-first or twenty-second. Although the primary focus is on Christmas, the western culture once celebrated the harvest, the solstice, Yule, and the return of the "Sun King."

Many of our ancestors were primitive and superstitious, but these same people also excelled in their ability to embrace nature's cycles. Despite months of darkness, bitter cold, and lack of fresh food, they kept light in their hearts and maintained faith that a healing sun would return in the spring. Few of us with the ability to read this book possess our ancestors' survival skills, natural knowledge, or perhaps even their spiritual wisdom. It may be possible to find similar equilibrium if we identify ways to challenge the stress placed on us by our technologically advanced era. Learning about the

MOTHER POT

past and incorporating practices to help us feel closer to those who lived before us could be the answer. There is much to explore, but historical evidence to guide us is often scant due to the ravages of nature or inequitable documentation by conquerors or indifferent cultures.

The Roman Empire maintained excellent records and their artifacts are well preserved, providing ample information about winter celebrations of that time. Conversely, we know less about Teutonic and Celtic practices because their oral history tradition and harsh climates adversely affected the preservation of evidence of cultural norms and artifacts. As a result, what we claim to know about cultures of these regions could be very wrong, and almost certainly cannot be proven. Experts agree that there is no irrefutable knowledge of the practice of ancient paganism in those particular areas.

Credible evidence points to overt manipulation, coercion, and disregard for indigenous beliefs by Christian authorities, though. Ancient paganism generally espoused a life-affirming perspective, including folk festivals characterized by respect and reverence for nature. Clearly, violent exceptions abound, and they are readily acknowledged in this book, but it was Christianity at its most rigid that proved to be the chief opponent of the gentler pagan perspective. Single-minded monks spread a philosophy that the fecund and rich earth was merely a place to show great discipline as a way to ensure entry into heaven. When the Church added countless items to the list of forbidden earthly delights, it is no wonder so-called heathens were slow, or often unwilling, to convert. Christian authorities continued to fight mightily against pagan rituals and relics, but eventually found it practical to allow some customs to continue—sanitized and purged of their original meaning. The result of this spotty intervention is a confusing collage of heathenism and Christianity we now recognize as modern Christmas.

It is not difficult to conclude that people once felt minimal boundaries between themselves and nature. To fully reclaim that perspective today may be impossible because doing so requires an impractical and eccentric lifestyle. Despite this limitation, we can tailor a collection of beliefs and rituals suitable for modern individuals, families, or groups of friends by collecting and incorporating into our lives artifacts and customs from our past. As our own organic philosophies evolve, this worthy effort may bind us together more richly than any contemporary technology. When musings about the past fuse with the broad mosaic of our

modern experience, we are ultimately rewarded with a unique and satisfying way to contemplate today's world.

Because so much pagan treasure has been neglected or intentionally purged from our culture, we must reclaim what we can, for our own sake, and for the benefit of generations to follow. Be bold in this effort. Confidently discard anxiety about appearing inaccurate or incorrect when honoring ancient ancestors. Emphasize instead how close to mother earth you feel, how alive, and how personally authentic your emotions are each time you light a candle, sing around a tree, or stand at the edge of a moonlit frozen pond on a frigid winter night. If the experience resonates, then the ritual or activity you have selected belongs in your own expanded belief system. Revel in a treasure of novel ideas for foods, rituals, crafts, music, or outdoor activities to fill the long winter season. Add these new pages to your life. Ultimately, it will not matter whether you have all the facts straight. It will matter that you feel whole.

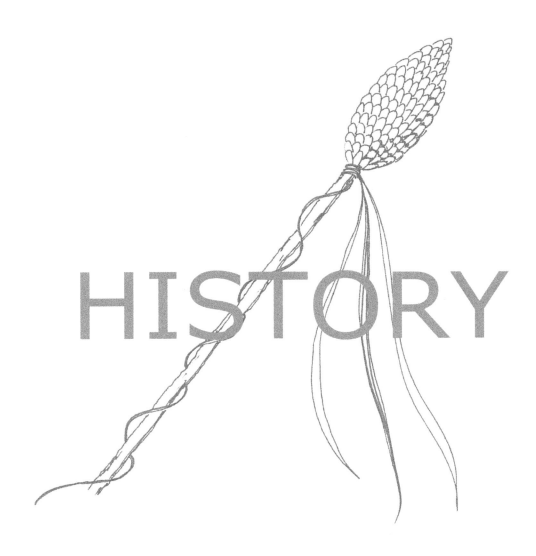

HISTORY

Staying Alive

It is cold and dark, and you are hungry. The wind is howling, and there is no way to stay warm. Savage animals growl outside your cave. The sun is weaker. The days are shorter. You wonder why.

Welcome to our religious roots.

Ancient humans had no concept of the winter solstice, the movement of the earth around the sun, or the tilt of the earth's axis, but by necessity, they were in sync with the seasons. A keen sense of sight, smell, and hearing often meant the difference between life and death. When the most intelligent individuals eventually detected seasonal patterns, confusion gave way to anticipation. They saw that light conquered darkness and winter eventually ended. Hope and faith were born.

Homo erectus discovered how to manage fire five hundred thousand years ago. Initially, he could only take fire from its source—a tree lit by lightning, volcanic activity, or natural gas—and attempt to harness it for his own needs. He could use it to drive animals from caves, then take residence there himself. If he took a bit of flame to his new cave, he could kindle and prolong it, until it eventually died out. Accidentally, or by trial and error, he eventually produced sparks to start a fire.

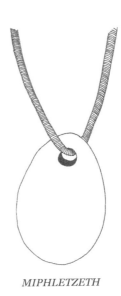

MIPHLETZETH

Suddenly, everything changed.

With this small step, nature can be seen in terms of action versus reaction. Some control over daily life is gained, at least in the ability to stay warm, see in the dark, and cook food. Family and clan members gather around a hearth to interact in an

> The goddess figure has endured over time.
>
> TONANTZIN *Mexican Corn Mother*
>
> HOLDA *Teutonic Earth Goddess of Fortune*
>
> BONA DEA *Roman Goddess of Abundance and Prophecy*
>
> OPS *Roman Goddess of Plenty*
>
> AU SET/ISIS *Egyptian All Goddess*
>
> MARY *Christian Mother of God*
>
> LUCIA *Roman/Swedish Goddess of Light*
>
> BEFANA *Italian Gift-Giving Witch*

exciting new way. With this primary need met, early humans moved onto higher levels of want and thought.

One new concept explored was the passage of time. As humans evolved, so did their understanding of time. Time was not a linear measurement for early man; it was a circular measurement, intimately bound to the seasons. Remnants of Paleolithic activity show us that people of the Early Stone Age focused on stories and events relating to seasons. Winter festivals were born of the realization that darkness would give way to light. Later, as an agricultural lifestyle evolved, the focus shifted to November's bountiful feasting.

Considerable attention was paid to the promise of fertility. The fecundity of women, animals, and land acquired new stature and reverence. Although remnants of ancient female fertility figures have been found over vast areas, it is unclear whether these figures were worshiped and actually represent the early seeds of religion. Regardless, focus on the female figure persisted, with it the veneration of a Mother Goddess figure, representing one of the most ancient and enduring components of a religion centered on the seasons.

Zagmuk

Although there is evidence of ceremonial burial by Neanderthals, and by inference, a belief in after-life, the first written documents about religious practices do not appear until approximately 3000 BCE. The Sumerians of Mesopotamia lived mostly in the area which is now modern Iraq. They recorded the oldest story in the world—The Epic of Gilgamesh—four hundred thousand years ago. Its hero was a bona-fide individual who ruled at a place named Uruk. In the Epic, a great flood annihilates all of mankind except one family who survives in the ark they built. On the ark of Gilgamesh are pairs of all animal species, as well as assorted artisans charged with preserving human knowledge. After the flood subsides, these people generate a new race to fill the world. Many historians believe the Epic of Gilgamesh provided the basis for the Bible story, Noah's Ark. Although there is no evidence to prove a catastrophic flood of this scale occurred, floods were a way of life in the Mesopotamian Delta. When the Tigris and Euphrates rivers flooded every spring, the Sumerians launched a week-long spring festival to celebrate the triumph of the regenerative forces of the earth and the beginning of a new year.

PAPIER MACHE MASK

The Babylonians succeeded the Sumerians, adopting most of their culture and social mores. Marduk, chief god of the Babylonians, is the revered hero of their creation myth, Enuma Elish. In this four thousand year old tale, Marduk visits the underworld to fight against the forces of evil on behalf of other gods. Victorious, he works to establish order out of chaos for the universe. He forms the heavens first, then earth, and finally, human beings. When bountiful fields wither after each harvest, it is Marduk who battles the evil powers of chaos as they try to gather strength. He ultimately wins, and the world is renewed once again.

To commemorate this, and to encourage another victory for Marduk, Babylonians performed a dramatization of the story of Enuma Elish at Zagmuk, their new year festival. Read aloud and reenacted, the epic further bolstered Marduk's dominance over the forces of evil. As their leader, the Babylonian king was designated as the one to die on Earth, then descend into the Underworld to aid Marduk. In the ensuing battle, this earthly king would die once again. A proxy common man with a spotted past was selected for the dubious honor to act as a mock king, sparing the real king's life. Dressed in royal garb, he was treated regally right up to the moment of his own sacrifice. Faux battles, bonfires, and gift exchanges followed this dramatization. Festivities stretched into a twelve day period of renewal during which participants strove to accomplish three things: receive absolution from the preceding year's sins, strengthen the embryonic new year, and identify a proxy person to suffer the consequences of collective sin.

A subsequent Babylonian/Persian annual renewal festival called Sacaea has less clear origins. One distinguishing feature was the practice of social inversion. Slaves exchanged places with masters. The Sacaea may have roots in the Babylonian custom of using a substitute king at Zagmuk. Much later, when Egyptian and Persian customs merged in Ancient Rome, many of these festival elements contributed to what became known as the Roman Saturnalia.

Aten Is Satisfied

Egyptians enjoyed rituals related to fertility, irrigation, and land reclamation, and fortunately for us, they kept excellent records. Rain, instead of sun, initiated their new year. After heavy precipitation, the Nile would flood and make the valley fertile for planting. In order to predict this occurrence, Egyptians tracked Dog Star Sirius as it moved across the night sky. After 365 days, Sirius reappeared on the eastern horizon in Memphis. Egyptians knew this meant the Nile's annual August flood was imminent.

During the Third Dynasty, Pharaoh Imhotep made several changes to this method of tracking time. Although a thirty-day lunar calendar already existed, Egyptians were challenged to integrate it into a 365 day year. Dividing the year into twelve months of thirty days each, they added the five leftover days to the end of the year. These unattached days spent waiting for Sirius to reappear on the horizon were treated as a festival. During this time, gifts such as scarabs were exchanged to celebrate the new year. Parents of deceased children placed puppets, small chariots, and various playthings on tombs in hopes of comforting the dead. Green date palm fronds were brought into homes. to summon the powers of nature and symbolize the triumph of life over death.

SUN-SHAPED SHORTBREAD

The god Osiris was the legendary ruler of pre-dynastic Egypt. His cult was one of the greatest in that region. Known as a benefactor of humanity, Osiris tamed men by music and gentleness, instead of force. He brought Egyptians knowledge of agriculture and civilization, and was both Lord of Fertility of the Nile River and Judge of the Dead. He was married to Isis, the great earth mother. Their son,

Horus, was the falcon-headed God of Light. According to historian Plutarch, Osiris was born on December twenty-seventh, the 361st day of the year. In the mythical tale, Osiris was killed by his brother Set, and later avenged by Horus, his son. Because Egyptian mythology says Osiris was resurrected, his birth was celebrated every year as part of the Isis and Osiris cult (approximately 2500–2001 BCE). Combined with the cults of Isis and Horus, the worship of Osiris spread throughout Mediterranean lands and became especially vibrant during the Roman Empire.

The pharaohs were revered above them all. As gods of earth, they controlled the Nile, while gods of heaven controlled the skies. It was Egyptian Pharaoh Amenhotep IV who decreed that only one god should exist, and that god should be Aten, symbolized by the solar disc. To show his devotion, Amenhotep IV changed his own name to Akhenaten, meaning, "Aten Is Satisfied."

Long before the birth of Jesus, Egyptians held a holiday on the date we know now as the sixth of January. They set aside this day to honor the Nile River, believing its water to then be most pure and optimal for use in holy ceremonies. When Christianity reached Egypt, the Egyptian Christians speculated that Jesus would have been baptized on this sacred date. Centuries later, Roman Church authorities selected December twenty-fifth as the best date to celebrate the birth of Jesus. The sixth of January became the Epiphany, the Twelfth Day of Christmas, and Three Kings' Day, when the three kings reportedly arrived in Bethlehem to visit the infant.

Beware the Kallikantzaroi

Records of Greek religion begin around 2000 BCE. In Greek mythology, Mother Earth Gaea rose from chaos, gave birth to Uranos (the sky), who later became her husband. Gaea and Uranos had many children, fourteen of whom became known as The Titans. After many years, the youngest Titan named Cronos led the others to rebel against their father, eventually deposing him. Ancient Greeks honored Cronos with the holiday named Kronia.

RHAMNA

Cronos married his sister Rhea. Their youngest son Zeus led his siblings in a successful revolt against the Titans and became the new leader. After Cronos fell, he fled to Italy, civilized its people, and developed agriculture. The other siblings moved to Mount Olympus and became known as Olympians.

Before embarking on projects, Greeks sought their gods' advice. They visited a special priest or priestess known as an oracle who could interpret the gods' desires. The word oracle has multiple definitions: a person who speaks for the god, a place where the priest or priestess could be consulted, or a message given to the advice seeker. In ancient Greece, the most famous and powerful oracle was the Delphic Oracle. The message of the oracle was spoken in an inner sanctuary by a priestess called the Pythia. She followed the ritual of bathing in a holy fountain, drinking water from a sacred spring, breathing smoke from burning laurel leaves, then lapsing into a deep trance. The Pythia's message was interpreted in verse spoken by a priest.

Later, in the sixth century BCE, Apollo's most prominent shrine in Delphi was established at the Delphic Oracle. Some historians believe that this shrine location represents a triumph of the cerebral perspective of Apollo over the earthy focus of the goddess. Prior to the Delphic Oracle, an earth goddess was worshipped at the

Greeks worshiped the pine tree in conjunction with Dionysus, God of Fertility and Wine. They used pine resin to conserve and refine wine, and even brewed wine from its seeds. Today, you can enjoy a popular resinated Greek wine called Retsina, made for over two thousand years.

same place. Evidence of remains of goddess worship has been found beneath the temple.

The god Dionysus was also worshiped at the Delphic Oracle, though to a lesser extent than Apollo. Dionysus was the god of wine. Representations show him holding an empty cup in one hand, and a vine staff in another. When the Delphic Oracle decreed that the Greek people should worship the pine tree in conjunction with Dionysus, evergreens became an important symbol of this worship. Because Greeks believed pine cones controlled the fecundity of land and womb, they were already established symbols of fertility within cults of female Greek goddesses.

Although Dionysus was also considered a god of fertility, this new designation was probably an attempt to divert focus from worship of the Earth Mother. Dionysus was originally a nature god whose cult complimented Apollo. Apollo was controlled and calculated, but Dionysus was characterized by abandon and lack of control. The combination of these two opposites more accurately reflects different aspects of human nature. The elevation of Dionysus dramatically eroded worship of the earth goddess, paving the way for the eventual appearance of the male-centered religion of Christianity.

The cult of Dionysus was celebrated during winter months. His festival was held on January fifth because Greeks believed this was the time of year when Apollo would be away from the Delphi

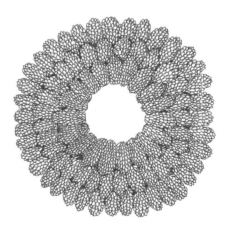

PINE CONE WREATH

temple. During this celebration, groups of young women called Maenads joined priests of Dionysus at a mountainous retreat. Oblivious to cold and harsh weather conditions, the group would perform sacred rites together, waving pinecone-tipped sticks called thyrsi in violent and frenzied ecstatic dancing. Animals that happened to be in their way were destroyed, and allegedly, humans as well.

Greeks believed the dimming light of winter encouraged ugly monsters of chaos called Kallikantzaroi to emerge from the bowels of the

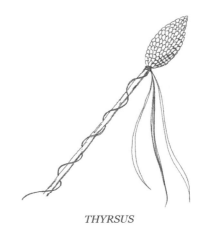

THYRSUS

Between Christmas and Twelfth Night, farmers gathered old leather shoes and burned them. The smell of burning animal hide was thought to be disagreeable to threatening spirits roaming the land.

earth. The Kallikantzaroi normally occupied themselves by sawing at roots of a great tree supporting earth and sky. The tree rapidly renews itself, endlessly infuriating the Kallikantzaroi. These malicious jokers emerge from the bowels of the earth to harass people, sour milk supplies, braid horses' tails, extinguish hearth fires, and create general nuisance. Conventional wisdom suggests that any child born during the Twelve Days of Christmas is in danger of becoming a Kallikantzaroi. As a preventative measure, baby's hair should be bound in garlic or straw, and his or her toenails singed.

Saturnalia

The number of religions practiced by Romans was as vast and varied as their empire. This included a collection of anthropomorphic gods, in which human shapes or characteristics are assigned to god, animal, or inanimate object. Because Christianity developed under the Roman Empire, many of our present practices can be traced back to this time.

In Greek mythology, Cronos fled to Italy after being ousted by his son, Zeus. He was befriended by Janus, king of the Romans, also known as the Latins. Cronos eventually married Ops, the Goddess of Plenty, and changed his ways. Instead of power, he sought peace of mind in the countryside of Italy,

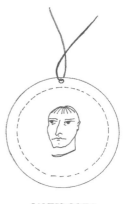

JANUS COIN

Artistic portrayals of Saturn, God of Sowing and Seed Corn, depict him as a bearded man carrying a sickle or an ear of corn. Somehow, the Romans confused the Greek god Cronus with the Greek word chronos, the word for time. The result is our image of Father Time, an aged bearded man holding a scythe.

focusing on the land and how best to use it for agriculture. He eventually became known as Saturn, a name derived from the word *satus*, meaning "to sow." Saturn and Janus joined forces, peacefully ruling the kingdom together. Romans believed Janus guarded the gates to the city of Rome, so Saturn thanked his friend for sharing his reign with him by giving Janus the ability to see both past and future. Because traffic moved both in and out of the gates, Janus is portrayed as having two faces: one looking forward, and one looking back. The name January is derived from the Latin word Janus, which means gate, or opening.

Saturn's reign was characterized by goodness and kindness of all people toward one another. No one in the realm fought or was jealous. The land they lived on was fertile and needed no cultivation to produce plentiful fruits and flowers. Legendarily, milk and nectar flowed through the meadow and honey flowed from trees. This idyllic time became known as the Golden Age.

> Romans believed the ivy plant prevented intoxication. For this reason, Bacchus, the Roman God of Wine and Revelry, is usually portrayed wearing ivy as a crown.

To commemorate this period, and to honor Saturn, the Romans held a festival called the Saturnalia, resembling the midsummer Greek holiday Kronia. This Roman festival occurred after the final harvest, prior to the beginning of the coldest season. It was originally confined to the seventeenth of December but gradually extended to seven days. Characterized by complete freedom of people and lack of customary societal rules, the Saturnalia encouraged relaxation of distinction between classes. Businesses, schools and courts were closed; people focused instead on enjoying themselves by abundant feasting and public gaming. Even soldiers stopped fighting and joined in merrymaking, ensuring a time of peace for all.

During the Saturnalia, many household slaves changed into their masters' clothing and wore soft caps called pileus, to signify their temporary liberation. They sat at tables with their masters, treating them as equals, or even inferiors. During this time, slaves were allowed freedom of speech, and could risk insulting their masters without fear for their lives. Occasionally, slaves were treated as superiors and served by their masters. Masters who felt this to be beneath their dignity instructed their children to wait on the slaves instead.

PILEUS CAP

Details of the Saturnalia changed over the hundreds of years it was celebrated, but its basic nature remained constant. On the first day, a pig was sacrificed. Meat was in good supply because animals were always butchered in early winter. With the harvest complete, there was also plenty of time to celebrate. Social mores shifted. Roman senators changed out of the power signifying toga into a peasant-like light dressing gown called the synthesis. All work was abandoned and revelry took over. No debts were collected and it was considered highly inappropriate for anyone to express anger or negative emotion during this festival period.

GLITTER CANDLES

Men and women moved through streets carrying lighted candles and garlands of greenery. Romans believed that if they exchanged green branches, good fortune would follow. They gathered "vervian," bunches of laurel, olive and myrtle, considered sacred to Strenia, Goddess of the Hearth. Romans affectionately gave this greenery to their rulers to wish them health and happiness, and perhaps to connect with the spirit of vegetation. They believed that the touch of a green branch would accomplish the same goal, so children set out to tap people with greenery and wish them good luck. People also decorated trees with small sculptures of Bacchus, Dionysus' Greek counterpart. Some trees were decorated with toys. A particularly beautiful display was a tree decorated with twelve candles topped with a likeness of the sun god.

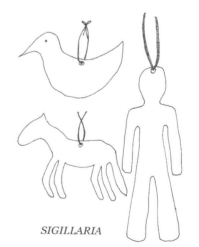

SIGILLARIA

Romans exchanged presents such as wax tapers called cerei, and tiny terra-cotta dolls called sigillaria. The cerei candles were given by the lower class to the upper class. The sigillaria were exchanged as friendly tokens, and are considered ancestors of our modern day greeting cards. Children played with these little dolls but adults used them as home decorations. Eventually, sigillaria were formed with pastry.

Gifts of money called sigillaria or saturnalicia were sometimes given in place of dolls. Other popular gifts at this time of year were lamps or luminaries decorated with a winged figure of Victory or laurel wreaths. Often, a Janus coin would be added to fruit and pots of money, all attractively arranged. These gifts are believed to be a remnant of an even more ancient festival of light held at the darkest time of the year when northern peasants burned a Yule log and made sacrifices.

PLASTER GAUZE MASK

Eastern Roman provinces selected a mock king for their festival. His job was to act as Saturn, providing comedy through his ridiculous antics. Some historians believe this mock king ritual is related to the ancient Mesopotamian Zagmuk festival, in which a king stand-in was sacrificed to ensure the renewal of the sun and seasons. At Saturnalia feasts, people wore loose garments made of bright material, or costumes with animal masks. Revelers danced in the streets, sang, drank, and were rowdy, similar to Mesopotamians who celebrated their new year when floods returned.

After the Saturnalia, a new holiday emerged. It was called Natalis Solis Invicti—Birthday of the Unconquerable Son. Emperor Aurelian's mother was a priestess from the Danube River region where sun worship had many adherents. Aurelian wanted to unite the various cults in the area by instituting a shared worship of the sun. According to the Roman calendar, December twenty-fifth was already the date of the winter solstice, and also fell conveniently between the Roman Saturnalia and the New Year. In 274 CE, Emperor Aurelian declared December twenty-fifth to be The Birthday of the Unconquerable Sun. This winter solstice feast honored the strength of the sun and the fertility it brought to the earth. As the Roman army spread its cult into Britain and other conquered areas, the festival meshed neatly with pre-existing celebrations honoring the rebirth of the sun at the winter solstice.

It was also a day to celebrate a god named Mithra, one of Christianity's strongest rivals. The worship of Mithra was known as Mithraism. Originating in Persia, it grew especially strong in the first century BCE. Mithra, whose name means friend, was a Persian deity of sunlight, fertility, and wisdom. His story may sound familiar. On the twenty-fifth of December during the fifth century BCE, Mithra was born of a virgin inside a cave. He had twelve companions. His two most important related festivals were the winter solstice and the spring equinox. Upon his death, he was buried in a tomb. He rose again—no longer mortal—now divine. Every year, his followers celebrated his rebirth by baptisms, honey anointments, as well as meals of blessed bread, water, and wine.

"Anno novo faustum felix tibi sit."

Traditional Roman New Year Greeting

GREETING

Mithraism is also similar to Christianity in that it is based on a belief in one god, has high standards of morality, a belief in judgment, a belief in life after death, and a Sunday Sabbath. Mithraism highlighted the eternal struggle between good and evil. Believers had a shot at immortality if they followed prescribed rules and rituals. It was a religion for men only and was especially popular with soldiers who were drawn to Mithra, God of Battle.

> Kalends is the root of the word calendar. In 153 BCE, the Romans began to use the first of January as a date to mark the beginning of the new year. Prior to this, the Roman new year was celebrated on the first of March.

The Saturnalia grew in length until it neared the date of the Roman New Year festival called The Kalends. The Kalends, or Calendae, was a three day festival that began on the first of January, also the first day of work for newly elected officials.

During the Kalends, Romans houses were illuminated and decorated with greenery of laurel and bay. The bay tree was believed to protect against fire or lightning. Presents, or strenae, were exchanged and given to the poor. Green branches, considered symbols of vitality, were given as gifts.

People greeted each other with the Latin phrase, "Anno novo faustum felix tibi sit"—"May the new year be happy and lucky for you." As the custom of gift giving grew to other regions, different varieties of greens were used. Olive, myrtle, rosemary, holly, ivy, and different fir tree boughs became popular. Eventually, wreaths and garlands were given instead of branches.

Because the main characteristic of the Kalends festival was generosity, the custom

PLASTER GAUZE MASK

of gift giving expanded. Romans were especially interested to learn what the coming year held for them, and believed gifts had power to affect their futures. Sweet gifts such as fruit, honey or mini-cakes brought sweetness to the future. Lamps decorated with symbols of good fortune heralded light and warmth. A full feast ensured a bountiful year. Gold and silver promised wealth. Nuts and dates, sometimes used like marbles by little boys, were also exchanged.

Notorious Emperor Caligula decreed that all high ranking officials give him money and more substantial gifts such as statuary, or crafts of gold and silver, during the festival. Eventually, money was commonly given as strenae (gifts). Singing children walked down streets, knocked on doors, and gave away coins. Recipients were encouraged to give children twice as many coins as they were offered.

The birth of Jesus and the spread of Christianity changed all of this, but not for quite some time, and not without calendar manipulation and edicts from powerful

Romans. For centuries, Jesus' birth was not celebrated in any way. The date was unknown and the event was not a focus of Christian worship. Speculated birthdates for Jesus were: January 1, January 6, March 25, and May 20. The late spring date was most popular because it was believed that angels delivering the good news to shepherds would have easily found them outside tending flocks in warm weather. The sixth of January eventually became known as the birthday of Jesus—a position held for centuries. If not his actual birthday, it was believed to be the day he was baptized, and therefore, the day of his divine birth. The actual date of his birth is still unknown.

> People in the Slavic and Baltic regions of Europe call their festivals variations of the word Kalends: Koleda, Kolyada, and Koledos.

There was conflict within the Church about whether Jesus could have been born both human and divine. In 245 CE, an influential Church official declared it a sin to have even a thought of celebrating the birth of Christ in the manner of a Pharaoh.

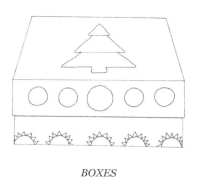

BOXES

Over a century later, in 353 CE, Pope Liberius solved the problem of Jesus' multiple birth dates by declaring that the birth of Jesus would be celebrated on the twenty-fifth of December. Veneration of the Light of the World would shift: the birth of the Son of God would replace the Birthday of the Unconquerable Sun. The impact was far reaching. Was the chosen date a deliberate and clever attempt by the pope to dilute focus on the Roman Saturnalia and Mithraism's Birthday of the Unconquerable Sun?

The new date was not welcomed by Syrian and Armenian Christians. They were scandalized by it. To them, it was more evidence of sun worship. They continued to honor the sixth of January as the birthday of Jesus, as stipulated by the Julian calendar.

Later, in the fifth century, Leo the Great was troubled by the continued intertwining of the birth of Jesus and the birth of the sun. He consequently banned most customs he believed were clearly pagan in character. He was unable to erase them all because many had already gone underground or were practiced only in the outer realm of the Roman Empire. In 601 CE, Pope Gregory confronted those who worshiped both Jesus and the sun. He ordered them to "no longer offer beasts to devils, but to worship God by feasting."

Ten centuries later, the Puritans would order Christians to fast instead of feast!

Murky Time

Around 1000 BCE, Germani tribes of Northwest Europe were migrating to the North German Plain, the Baltic Islands, and the region later known as Denmark. They were ancestors of Germans, Franks (French), and Angles and Saxons (British). The group of Germani who moved into Scandinavia were called North or Norse men. From 700 CE to 1070 CE, these people were known as Vikings.

With their magical stories about trolls, elves, and fairies, Norse customs related to the winter solstice convey a sense of a very ancient time. In Scandinavia, winter is not only cold and long, it is oppressively dark. In fact, the Norwegian name for winter is Mørketiden (mur-ka-tee-den), "the murky time." During this season, great Viking seafarers were unable to sail, so rich storytelling sustained them through long winter nights.

WINTER SOLSTICE MOBILE

Nothing about Norse history or their myths was written down until around the twelfth century CE, when it was duly recorded by a Christian. The philosophical perspective of the recorder was at odds with the Viking religion, so it likely affected story transcription. Conversion of Norse people to Christianity was a long process, and most Vikings did not convert until forced by their kings, often under torture. One of the more hideous methods purportedly used to make an example of those who refused to convert was to place a snake headfirst inside a hollow stick, then place the stick between the martyr's teeth. The snake would slide down into the man's stomach, eating its way out. Death would be excruciatingly slow and painful.

Around 1000 CE, the people of Iceland were forced to embrace Christianity. They agreed to do so only if they could continue to make private sacrifices to their Viking gods. This was promised, but a short time later, rescinded.

Retaining some Roman influence, Germanic people named days of the week.

Sunday Sun's Day

Monday Moon's Day

Tuesday Tiw's Day for Tiw/Tyr, God of War

Wednesday Woden's Day for Woden/Odin, Supreme God, King of the Gods. Woden was chief of the Germanic gods. His name was pronounced Odin in Scandinavia. Sharp-eyed ravens sat on each of his shoulders. Two ravens spent their time flying over the earth, reporting to Woden all they saw. Woden traveled the world on Sleipner, a white horse with eight legs whose speed exceeded that of a four legged horse. Some believe that this image of Woden evolved into the character we know as Santa Claus.

Thursday Thor's Day for Thor, God of Thunder. The oak tree was sacred to Thor. He was always shown with his symbol—the hammer—on which his strength depended. The sign of the hammer was used by his cult to ward off danger. The Roman Catholic Christian cross symbol resembles it.

Friday Frigg's Day for Frigg, Mother Goddess Queen of the Heavens. Frigg is also the wife of Woden. She was the symbol of fertility, prosperity, peace, and sensuous love.

Saturday Saturn's Day

Norse winter customs are derived from rich mythology. At the center of this mythology is an ash tree called Yggdrasil, known also as World Tree or Tree of the Universe. It is where Norse gods live. It is considered the tree of life because all of Nature flows from and thrives because of it. The tree features nine, three-level worlds. The gods and goddesses live on the highest level, where water from a fountain preserves the area and represents seasonal revival. A rainbow bridge connects this upper level to the middle level, the Earth. The lowest level contains the Land of the Dead where a dragon gnaws at its root, symbolizing seasonal decay.

The father of all of the Norse gods is Odin, also known as Woden or Jolnir, creator of the Earth and sky and all living creatures. He is a respected and feared god of battle. He has a long white beard. Woden is also god of drink and ecstasy. His wife Frigg is Queen of the gods and Mother goddess to all. Together they have a son named Balder who is loved by everyone. The kind, gentle, and wise Balder is the god of light, purity, and beauty.

Balder begins to dream about death. The truth of these nightmares is confirmed by a seeress who says his death is unavoidable. In an effort to prevent his premature demise, Balder's mother Frigg compiles a list of everything in the lands of Yggsdrasil that can possibly harm Balder, ordering all to pledge never to hurt him. Mistletoe is the only plant she overlooks. Meanwhile, a god named Loki has grown more and more jealous of Balder. Disguised, Loki learns about the mistletoe omission from Frigg, finds some of the plant, and then makes an arrow out of it. In a cruel twist, Loki manages to trick Balder's blind brother Hod into shooting this arrow, ultimately killing Balder. When Loki's mother learns of his death, she cries, and her tears turn into white berries as they fall onto the mistletoe. These berries come to symbolize love that is stronger than death.

> Roman mythology revered mistletoe because it was believed to contain the seed of fire. A branch of it became known as the Golden Bough when Aeneas carried it to light his way through the underworld of Hades. Other anecdotal benefits attributed to mistletoe, also known as Allheal are poison antidote; fertility promoter; protection against premature birth; cure for epilepsy; and ulcer healer. The people of Northern European countries believed that if two enemies stood together beneath mistletoe, they would become friends. (Note: Mistletoe has varying degrees of toxicity to both humans and pets.)

Mistletoe assumes a new power. It will now act as a protector and ensure peace and friendship after being ordered to never again harm anyone. Norse people honored this tradition by forming truces when enemies met under mistletoe. They would surrender their weapons maintain peace for the duration of the day. Mistletoe once hung in Norse houses all year as a sign that guests who entered underneath it were safe while in that house. Mistletoe grows on apple, poplar, lime, mountain ash, hawthorn, maple, and laurel, but rarely on oak.

> Pre-Christian Sweden celebrated Midvinterblot, or Midwinter Blood, a ritual sacrifice of animals and humans at secret cult locations. Their hope was that these sacrifices would encourage local gods to loosen their grip on winter. Many Swedish churches are built over these sacrificial sites.

According to the ancient Norse calendar, the thirteenth of December was believed to be the longest night of the year and consequently considered a most dangerous night. Creatures from the underworld and spirits of the dead wandered in the dark. On the night of the winter solstice, Odin would leave Valhalla, the place of the souls of the dead, mount his eight-footed horse Sleipnir, and join other gods to hunt evil-doers on Earth. The midwinter high feast to honor Odin and to recognize other dark ancestral spirits was called Ialka tid, Joulu, Jol or Yuletide.

> Human and animal sacrifice horrifies us today. Why not make an effort to redirect related energies of the past by doing something positive for humankind during the Midvinterblot season? Donate blood to your community blood bank.

Yule was a twelve day festival to honor the sun as it regained strength and overcame the darkness of winter. The precise origin of the festival remains unknown but it occurred during the coldest of Germanic seasons, starting mid-November and ending mid-January. There were plentiful feasts of food and drink. One of the featured foods was the sacred wild boar. The Norse believed that although the gods at Yggdrasil ate the Sun Boar every night, the boar grew whole again each morning. In later times, the Norse baked a dough Yule boar called Julgalt on Christmas Eve. A piece was reserved, dried, and kept until spring to be fed to the horse and to those who worked the plow. It was thought to act as a charm to improve the new season's crop.

After feasting, the Norse donned scary costumes and took to the streets to frighten monsters. They stopped at homes along the way where they were given a type of brandy called "lussesup," the drink of light. "A Glad Yule!" was the customary greeting to all, and only the most necessary work was done during the festival. The use of wagons, spinning wheels and anything else with a wheel was prohibited during this time. It was a grave offense to the sun to let any wheel move because this indicated a wish for the wheel of the sun to move at a quicker pace. Finally, at the end of the twelve days, an enormous wheel was rolled between farms to celebrate the lengthening days.

ST. LUCIA ROLLS

The Norse believed that winter was a time when ancestral spirits returned to walk the Earth. Many details of their celebrations are related to this belief and how best to welcome these spirit guests. The house should be spotless before the family heads to church in the evening because spirits are certain to visit and inspect everything, as well as sample the food. In some parts of Northern Sweden, a specific table is designated for visiting spirits. If good relations are kept with the spirit world, the upcoming year will also be good.

Norse Yule was also a time to honor animals. It was considered important for them to experience a most peaceful existence during these twelve days. No traps could be set, and fishing was prohibited. Humans, animals, birds, and fish were to have complete peace. The best sheaves of wheat or barley were put aside at harvest time and mounted on tall poles to ward off evil spirits during the darkest nights of winter. Norwegians made a bird pole out of a spruce tree, leaving a few branches at the top. They tied sheaves of grain around the base, then put it in the middle of a large circular area cleared of snow. Pieces of suet were attached to the limbs of trees as well. The Swedes spread pieces of juniper or spruce on their parlor floors, creating a delicious fragrance in their homes. Sometimes straw was strewn about to appease the corn spirit. Ancient Swedes believed that straw saved from the last Yule contained corn spirit and could act as a fertility charm.

JULBOK

Straw is a major decorating material for Swedes. A straw goat called a "Julbok" appears in almost every home around this time of year. Large Julboks are placed under Christmas trees and little ones are found on tabletops.

The Julbok is one of a variety of straw animals called Jul-cocka. Originally, the Julbok was designed to represent the sacred goat of Thor, the Norse god of thunder. Straw was used to make the goat because it was symbolic of grain and representative of food and prosperity. Yule pigs called Julgrisar were also made by the Norse. The pig represented the massive wild boar that pulled fertility god Frey in his chariot. Frey was also god of light and peace and caused the earth to be fruitful. In Norway, straw figures of people and animals were hidden in lower branches of trees to symbolize spirits believed to be living in the grain.

> During religious ceremonies, a man dressed in a goatskin and goat mask carried the Julbok. This practice was later banned by both Catholic and Protestant churches because of the goat's association with devil worship.

The custom of the Yule Log originated with the Norse and was related to the worship of Yggdrasil. The log was usually an enormous trunk of an ash tree. Sometimes more than a log—it was occasionally an entire tree. One end would be stuck into the fireplace and the other end would jut out into the room. As the log burned, the outside end would be pushed toward the fire. It was often bound with as many shoots of twisted hazel as possible because ash and hazel trees were sacred

to the Norse. When each hazel binder burned through, a quart of cider was drunk by the surrounding folks. As long as the fire burned, the merriment and good will continued. It was supposed to smolder on the hearth for twelve days.

Norse believed that evil fears light, so when a fire burned in

> In Denmark, New Year's Eve is a time of merriment and mischief. Besides the usual "ring and run" prank at local houses, country children relish another practice. They spend the fall collecting broken pottery bits to use on New Year's Eve, when they throw pieces at the doors of all of their favorite neighbors. This noisy ritual is intended to scare away evil and discourage spirits from entering homes. The unwelcome would first have to cross broken pieces of crockery strewn over steps.

the hearth, no evil would dare enter through the chimney. An old Norse legend says that Hertha, goddess of home and domesticity, would descend through the smoke and appear in the fireplace. This would forecast good luck for that home.

> Norse believed that mistletoe gave them good luck and also increased fertility. It was the plant of peace because enemies became friends when they stood together beneath it.

Evergreens represented eternal life to the Norse. Mistletoe, ivy, holly, box, bay, juniper, rosemary, spruce, and pine could protect from evil spirits. Mistletoe in particular was revered by the Norse because of its connection to the death of Balder. The Celtic Druids also honored it. Mistletoe was known as the legendary Golden Bough. It was known as Allheal in folk medicine because it was used as a cure for numerous ailments, including an antidote for poison. Mistletoe is poisonous, so the healing power was in the magic, not in the medicinal use of the plant.

A Yule candle accomplished two critical needs of the season: illumination and warmth. This enormous candle is purportedly a phallic derivative. Whatever its

origin, different countries had different customs related to it. Many Norse lit the candle on Christmas Eve and extinguished it on Christmas Day at sunrise. In Denmark, two huge candles were used; one was for the master of the house and one for the mistress of the house. In Norway, the candle was relit each evening until New Year's Day. The oldest member, or head of household, was designated to put out the flame. It was considered bad luck to touch the Yule candle in any other way after

YULE CANDLE

it was lit, or to let it burn out before the end of the evening. The custom of the Yule candle was once widespread, but today it is most often seen in the form of electric candles decorating windows during the Christmas season.

Later in history, the thirteenth of December was distinguished from the rest of Yule when it became known as the great Christian festival of Advent called St. Lucia's Day, also known as Little Yule. Its history is rooted in the festival of lights but as Christianity took hold, the pagan aspect diminished. St. Lucia was a

CANDLE CROWN

Sicilian Christian woman put to death by Emperor Diocletian on December 13, 304 CE. Lucia was engaged to be married but gave her dowry to the poor folk of the village instead of her fiancé's family. Her prospective husband felt that this was surely a Christian act. Since it was illegal to be a Christian, he promptly turned her over to the proper authorities in Rome, where she was sentenced to die.

Legend says that during a horrible December famine, a peasant experienced a vision of a white robed Lucia wearing a circle of glowing lights on her head, and carrying a tray of food. When this vison was retold, it was seen as a sign that the famine had ended. Lucia is also credited with bringing food to her fellow prisoners every night. She wore candles on her head in order to keep her hands free to carry food. Another legend says that as she was burned at the stake, flames would not harm her. She died only after someone drove a sword through her. Stories of Lucia were probably brought to Sweden by Christianized Viking traders.

On St. Lucia's Day, a village selects a Lucia Queen or Lucia Bride who dresses all in white, often with a red sash. She wears a crown of whortleberry twigs and greenery with nine flaming candles in it. Rising before sunrise, the queen leads a procession of girls and boys as she visits homes where she offers coffee and pastries. Her appearance illustrates a promise that light will return and the Earth will provide for all. Girls who accompany the Lucia Queen dress as maids of honor, and boys dress as trolls and other monsters that the returning sun has conquered.

SILVER GARLAND CORONET

In private homes, either the youngest or oldest daughter acts the part of the Lucia Queen. She rises before sunrise wearing her white costume and wakes her family, serving them hot beverages and pastries. Other children wear long white robes; the girls wear crowns made of silver tinsel and the boys wear white cone shaped hats. Special songs are sung as they sit together on their parents' bed. Flattened saffron-colored Lusse rolls are served.

Some families enjoy stars and hearts made out of gingerbread as well. A more substantial breakfast is offered later in the morning in the home's most brightly lit room. Even pets are included in the joy of celebrating the sun's rebirth with lavish quantities of food.

CONE HAT

Ancient Swedes believed that little men with long grey beards called tomtens lived in dark corners under boards around their farms. The tomten, generally considered a benign resident of the farm, would become destructive if ignored. Particularly mischievous during the winter season when dangerous spirits were afoot, he could be calmed by leaving out offerings of food and drink. Over time, and due to Christian influence, his image softened and he became known as one who watched over farm and family. He began to give, rather than receive gifts, eventually resembling the role of Santa Claus. The tomten hid little packages for children throughout the house.

Rich rice pudding made with raisins and cinnamon is presented as a first course during Christmas Eve dinner. A single almond is stirred into the pot before serving. The recipient of the almond is treated as royalty for the entire evening, with added assurance of good luck in the coming year.

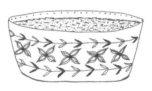

RISPUDDING

A bowl of rice pudding was also placed in a farmyard or garden to placate the ancient little gnome-like men called Nisser. These twist-bearded gnomes dress all in red and wear smocks and little clogs. Stories about the Nisser are over four thousand years old. They are portrayed as spirits of ancestors who control family destiny and finances. Nisser of today have been sanitized and softened.

Prior to modern Christmas, the Norse gift giver was a goat. Gift givers dressed as goats before the time when Father Christmas became accepted in this region. As

Christianity developed, the goat image became associated with Satan. The Church would not tolerate the connection, so this gift giving custom gradually disappeared.

Gift giving in Sweden today is characterized by the charming custom of attaching a card featuring an original rhyme with a hint about the package's contents. Gifts are traditionally wrapped in white paper and red bows. The paper is sealed with sealing wax. The smell of burning sealing wax evokes many warm feelings to those who once wrapped presents this way.

The Julkapp gift is an interesting custom in Sweden and northern Germany. The idea is to wrap a gift in an abundance of paper so that no one can guess its contents. The one who delivers the Julkapp can be male or female, but must be unexpected. He or she quickly opens the door,

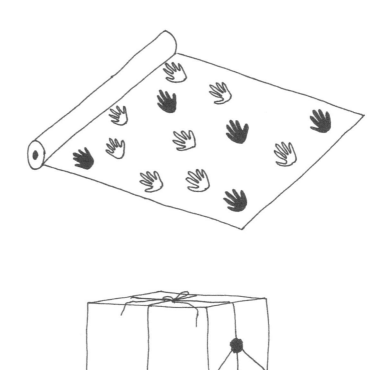

throws the gift inside, and then escapes unrecognized. A variation on this delivery is the arrival of two people disguised as an old man and old woman who ring a bell outside a home. When occupants open the door, they are greeted by the couple who hold a basketful of presents. The origin of surprise gift giving, like many ancient customs, is unknown.

Norse Yule ends on the thirteenth of January, Saint Knute's Day. King Knute (or Canute) ruled over Norway, Denmark, and England one thousand years ago. He declared that Yule feasting should last from the twenty-fifth of December until the thirteenth of January. On the last day, parties to take down the tree are held. People of all ages wear party hats and sing and dance to drive out Yule.

> Danes signaled farmhands and neighbors that the house was ready for Christmas by placing sheaves of wheat outside and hanging a pinecone wreath on the door. Homemakers decorated with red paper garlands, and displayed gnome and goblin figurines in the kitchen.

After all decorations have been removed from the tree, it is thrown out of the window. In earlier times, both master of the house and servants would participate in a mock fight by using kitchen tools and implements to drive away leftover guests. Everyone sings:

"The twentieth day,

King Knut did rule

Would end the festival of Yule."

In Northern Norway, a holiday called Soldag is celebrated. Since the sun does not reappear there until early February, there is great celebrating when it does. On any given day during the time of the sun's first reappearance, school teachers may announce to the children that the day has been declared Soldag or Sun Day. Children are consequently allowed to spend the day outdoors at play.

> Danish children believe that a gnome called Jule-nissen brings them gifts. To keep his favor, they set out a generous serving of rice pudding on the night he is expected to arrive.

In southern Norway, there is a town called Rjukan situated in a deep valley. Until recently,* its residents did not see the sun from the fifth of October until the twelfth of March. When it finally appears, a Sun Pageant is held. Everyone congregates in the town square, wearing creative masks and costumes over bulky winter clothing. All around them are sparkling columns of ice topped by fiery torches. A preselected Prince of the Sun appears. Dressed in medieval costume, he walks around the square. Young women, dressed in white gowns and tall, cylindrical hats and veils surround him. The Prince approaches his throne on a platform in front of a dark blue backdrop accented with a painting of a large yellow sun. He turns to the crowd, proclaiming, "Let there be merriment until dawn!" Festival activities include costume contests, magic acts, clowns, acrobats and abundance of food. Eventually, the Prince orders everyone to remove their masks, revealing revelers' identities. A display of fireworks brings the party to an end.

Christian missionaries recorded many ancient tree trimming rituals that accompanied winter solstice celebrations. In northernmost parts of Norway called Lapland, as well as in Sweden and Finland, a tiny detailed boat was constructed and filled with small amounts of foods served at the solstice feast. The boat was placed among branches of a designated pine tree that had been previously marked on four sides with sacred symbols. In another pine tree, the internal organs of a freshly killed reindeer were hung, and the tree was smeared with animal blood.

*In 2013, a series of computerized solar-powered mountain-top mirrors were installed to redirect sunlight into the valley of Rjukan.

Dwarves, Elves, Sprites, and Spirits

Central Europe is where customs from surrounding regions blend, creating the interesting hodgepodge we generally recognize today as Christmas. Practices of northern Europe (Scandinavia) and southern Europe (Roman Empire) merged. Teutonic people (Anglo Saxon, German, Dutch, Austrian, and Scandinavian) and Slavic (Russian, Polish and some people of southeastern Europe) influenced the outcome. Because they communicated their beliefs with legends, rituals, and songs, there is little concrete evidence about these ancient people. They left no enduring monument—such as a pyramid—to withstand the Roman invasion. They favored sacred groves and hilltops as places of worship. Their religion was simple and free of the complex hierarchy and institutionalization that ultimately characterized Christianity.

 For the most part, these people worshiped gods of nature. Primary deities were accompanied by a rich family of dwarves, elves, sprites, and spirits, adding a colorful dimension to believers. The dark side of European paganism lies in the horrific acts of animal and human sacrifice. This attribute, not unique to the region, is often used as a reason to condemn paganism.

Although it is difficult to definitively determine what rituals were practiced, several sources have helped scholars piece together information. Records from Rome and Greece are abundant, but historians are cognizant that chroniclers of history suffer from conflicts of interest, and lack the perspective of the native psychology. Even so, Christianity provides one of the best sources of data. The pagan practices surviving within Christianity reinforce origins that have been well entrenched.

Folklore offers scholars an additional information source, but its validity is compromised by the challenge to distinguish essence from embellishment.

Pagan festival season extends from the first of November (All Saints Day) to the sixth of January (Epiphany). According to the lunar calendar, a day begins at sundown. For this reason, pagan and non-Christian holidays traditionally commence at sundown on the day prior to the actual holiday. This practice of starting a holiday in the evening persisted even after the switch to the solar calendar.

NATURE CROWN

Teutonic and Celtic calendars made no mention of a solstice feast, and there is no concrete evidence that the winter solstice was celebrated in any way. The focus of the season was primarily practical. When the earth could no longer provide food for grazing animals, the livestock had to be slaughtered. Feasting likely began when the first snowfall covered pastures in the middle of November. The availability of other fresh meat was restricted to cold months when natural refrigeration held off decay until meat could be salted for long term storage. As farming methods improved, the need to slaughter animals was pushed further ahead in the calendar, and surplus hay could be fed to animals weathering the season in their stalls. Farmers could finally see the culmination of a season's work and anticipate a period of relaxation. Since the supply of beer and wine was also ready for sampling, general celebration was a natural outcome.

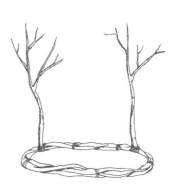

ANTLER CROWN

Jiuleis, Giuli, or Yule occurred in the most northern regions of Europe, as it did in Scandinavia. Great quantities of meat were available for a feast that was characterized by numerous fires, fire rites, and attempts to honor and soothe spirits of dead ancestors. At these enormous bonfires, excited young men tried to leap over flames. Men and women cross-dressed similarly to the way they did during the Saturnalia.

ANIMAL COSTUME

Apple or oak Yule logs, ideally with their massive roots retained, were selected months before the feast, allowing sufficient time to properly dry out and consequently burn brighter. There was much ceremony around bringing this Yule log to the home. Following prescribed rituals assured protection from witchcraft in the year to come. Some people sat on the log one at a time and sang a song before giving the log a kiss. Wine was often sprinkled over it as wishes for good health and happiness for the household were spoken.

YULE LOG CENTERPIECE

In Yugoslavia, corn and wine were thrown on the log to ensure a bountiful harvest. In Bulgaria, the father carried a log inside by himself, and everyone tossed corn and wine at him. Slavic, Croatian, and Serbian women and girls wound red silk and gold wire around the felled trunks of oaks, adding flowers and leaves as a finishing touch. The log carrier would often place an orange, some corn, and the blade of a plough on the log to encourage the health of domestic animals and the spring crop. In some homes, wine was poured over a piece of unleavened bread situated on top of the log.

Also in Yugoslavia, a boy called the "polaznik" entered homes early Christmas morning and threw a handful of wheat on each resident. He tapped the Yule log while expressing wishes of good luck, prosperity, progress, and happiness to everyone, including family livestock. When he sat on the floor to ground his wishes, his hosts wrapped a thick blanket around him to ensure a good supply of thick cream in the coming year.

There was also great ceremony around lighting the fire and watching the Yule log burn. The fire must be lit with clean hands. Once burning well, the head of household assured those gathered around that the bright flames would drive hatred from them. The Yule log was believed to have mystical qualities. It could guard a home against spirits and keep peace in relationships between family and friends.

> Ashes are beneficial to soil. Scatter Yule ashes in your own garden and let them work modern day magic.

When the feast ended, a piece of charred yule log remains would be salvaged. Often stored at home until the next year, it was tucked under a bed to give special protection from fire and lightning. Many believed that the Yule log remnant had many special qualities. It could protect people from chilblains. When mixed with grain and fed to cows, it was believed to increase fertility. An unburned part of log was often formed into a plow section and used to increase the fertility of seeds. After next year's log was brought into the home, the old piece was used as kindling for the new Yule fire. Ashes from the Yule log were collected and spread around fruit tree roots and scattered on farm fields to improve fertility.

> There are other names for the Yule log.
> *Eastern Europe*: Badnjak.
> *France:* Souche de Noel, Chalendal, Calignaou, Tre'fouet, Tre'foir, Tison de Noel.
> *Italy*: Ceppo Suc, Zocco, Ciocco, di Natale.

There are different interpretations surrounding the tradition of the Yule log. Some believe the oak log itself was a symbol of the spirit of vegetation and the burning of it representative of the power of sunshine and warmth. The log could have been burned to honor the hearth, the center of family life. The concept of fire was also associated with the spirits of ancestors.

Teutonic tribes gradually migrated into southern areas of Central Europe, as well as Britain and Gaul. In these warmer regions, the first signs of winter appeared later in the year. Consequently, celebration of the Yule festival occurred during December and January when everything was at its darkest.

People in Roman occupied regions influenced by the Natalis Solis Invictis, the Saturnalia, and Yuletide, combined these rituals with great feasts that included fertility worship and the cult of the dead. With more diverse observances from different cultures—Nordic, Teutonic, Celtic, Greek, and Roman—the concept of Yule became richer than ever. Because deeply rooted ancient Yule rituals could not be eliminated, they eventually blended into a multicultural celebration of Christmas.

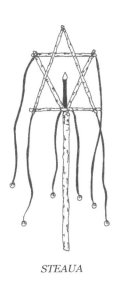

STEAUA

Northern Europeans tied gilded apples to trees to honor their god Odin/Woden, supplier of the fruits in life. They also hung animal, bird, and fish-shaped little cakes from branches. European kitchen maids with hands full of sticky Christmas pie dough were encouraged to go out into orchards and hug a fruit tree to encourage its fertility. On Christmas Eve, there was a custom of knocking with bent fingers on a tree, asking the tree to wake up.

On Christmas Eve in Serbia, the head of household lit a candle that had been placed in a shallow box of wheat. Everyone prayed for good crops and general well-being for the family in the coming new year.

In Eastern Europe, Christmas was primarily a feast of the dead. Remains of the Christmas meal were left out for three days so that spirits of the house could help themselves. They believed that ancestral spirits often lived underneath the doorway of a home.

Attention was paid to the fire in the hearth where rituals took place to honor ancestors. One requirement was the removal of fire irons, tables, and chairs or stools from the room before the Yule log entered the house. Some historians believe this indicates that these ceremonies were ancient, and derived from a time when such household items did not yet exist.

From primitive times, people hung greenery in their homes as a refuge for wood spirits. They believed spirits left their homes in the trees during the pagan winter feast and drifted around in the cold dark night. By providing safe haven, it was hoped that one day spirits would return the favor and bring them good luck.

Early European pagans worshipped trees as objects, but this practice eventually evolved into a worship of the spirit perceived to live in a tree.

GERMAN LICHSTOCK

Long ago, a ceppo—Italian word for tree trunk—was burned at the winter celebration. Blindfolded children were given sticks and encouraged to hit the burning trunk and make special wishes. With blindfolds removed, children found gifts for themselves on the ground. This custom eventually evolved into the pyramid,or Lichstock, its shape reminiscent of a tree or flames rising.

Greenery found a special place in their celebrations. The presence of it inside the home during winter is traced back to the ancient Egyptians practice of date palms adorning home interiors.

A German custom called "peppering" (pfeffern) has pre Christian roots. On the twenty-sixth of December, girls "beat" their parents and godparents with branches of green fir. The following day, boys take their turn. Male servants "beat" their masters with sticks of rosemary. After chanting, "Fresh green! Long life!" they are treated to assorted goodies such as plum loaf, gingerbread, and brandy. Men use birch rods to "whip" women and girls in bed, singing, "Fresh green, fair and fine, gingerbread and brandywine." The next day, women do the same to men. Similar to the Roman ritual, the intent of the whipping is not to inflict pain, but to chase away bad spirits. It is a transfer of the sacred plant's good qualities to the person touched by it.

Some Europeans brought branches of evergreens into their homes, decorated them, and hung them from ceilings. A branch from a cherry or hawthorn tree was clipped in the fall, placed in water, and brought into the house to provide early winter blossoms. On the last day of November, Romanian mothers collected

> Holly represents eternal life and hospitality. Broadcast this goodness by stuffing little sprigs of holly behind mirrors and paintings hung on your walls.

small branches from fruit trees and tied individual bunches together to represent each child in the family. The sprays were placed in water and monitored to see which would bloom first. The corresponding child was promised good luck in the year to come.

POLISH DINNER WREATH

A beautiful medieval custom was to spread rosemary on the floor of the great hall. When guests walked over the herb, spicy fragrance was released into the air. This was especially welcomed because the smell of rosemary was believed to preserve the youth of revelers. In Poland, peasants spread straw on their tables, then covered it with a table cloth over which they prepared the seasonal feast. Some of the straw or hay was spread on the floor as well. Later, these sanctified cuttings were fed to animals in the barn, or scattered around fruit trees to influence their yield. In some European homes, a sheaf of wheat was placed in each corner of a room. At the end of the holidays, these sheaves were distributed over fields in hopes of a good harvest, and also to provide feed for birds.

OXEN ROLLS

Bay, laurel, ivy, holly, and mistletoe were all used to decorate interiors, but holly, ivy, and mistletoe were considered especially significant because they bore winter fruit. Some evergreens—especially holly—were believed to have supernatural powers. Holly symbolized joy, peace, domestic happiness, foresight, friendship, and good wishes. It was thought to ward off witches and protect a home from lightning, if planted nearby. Plentiful holly berries on a bush forecast a severe winter. A holly sprig placed on a bedpost encouraged pleasant dreams. In ancient times, holly was hung in churches to welcome elves and fairies. In Rome it was a symbol of good will and often offered as a gift during the Saturnalia, and at weddings as a congratulatory token. Domestic animals were thought to thrive if holly was hung in their stalls within view.

In some European regions, holly was used to forecast the future. Holly leaves with tiny candles on them were floated on water. Sinking leaves meant a project was doomed. It was important

The Epiphany, or Twelfth Night, was a time to eradicate evil spirits. Boys in Switzerland set out with torches, bells and horns, making a great racket to scare away malicious spirits of the woods. In Germany, on the eve of Epiphany (Bergnacht), boys and girls ran through streets knocking loudly on doors in an attempt to chase away evil spirits. In the eastern Alps, large crowds of young men dressed in wild masks, and armed with cowbells, whips, and weapons, ran around and shouted with abandon.

to consider what variety of holly to bring into the home for Christmas decorations. The smooth type meant a wife would rule the house all year; the prickly kind meant a husband would. Although it was a popular decorative plant, it was considered an encouragement to goblins if left in the home after New Year's Day, or at the latest, Twelfth Night. Over three hundred species of holly are spread throughout the world.

"Wraeth" is the Anglo Saxon origin of the word wreath. It means twisted band. Wreaths represent eternal life and symbolize victory and glory. They were often used as the focus of magic. Wreaths were even found in pharaoh tombs in Egypt.

The Christmas tree is believed to be the winter equivalent of the May Tree or Maypole, both symbols of fertility. These seasonal symbols are also related to Yggdrasil—the Norse Tree of Life—and Sakai, the tree Japanese worshipped along with their sun goddess. The European Yule tree was an undecorated live tree planted in a bucket of dirt brought into the home during the festival days. The German Carol "O Christmas Tree" illustrates the reverence and joy surrounding their tree.

O Christmas Tree! Fair Christmas Tree!

A type of life eternal!

O Christmas Tree! Fair Christmas Tree!

Your boughs are ever vernal.

So fresh and green in summer heat,

And bright when snows lie round your feet.

O Christmas Tree! Fair Christmas Tree!

CANDLE WREATH

A type of life eternal!

When it is was impossible to have a tree in the home, some Europeans built a wooden form called a pyramid. This was particularly popular with the upper middle class. This pyramid, decorated with colored paper, as well as candles or green twigs, was saved to use year after year. Early in the 1800s, pyramids featuring a layer of gilt evergreens covered with apples and nuts were frequently given away as gifts.

In sections of Germany and Austria, only the tip of the evergreen was used as a home decoration. Hung upside down from the rafters, it was decorated with apples, gilded nuts, and pieces of red paper.

What would a festival be without food? Wild boar was a food revered by Europeans and Norse. This dangerous and fierce hog once roamed the forests of Europe. It was believed to be sacred to the god Frey and became his symbol. The boar had special significance because it stuck its tusks into the earth like a plow. It was ritualistically sacrificed to ensure good weather and good crops.

In the Middle Ages, roast peacock was another popular dish. The bird was plucked and skinned prior to cooking. After it was cooked, the feathers were meticulously reapplied, with tail plumage spread for full effect. The beak was often gilded, stuffed with a cloth soaked in liquor, then set aflame. When it was brought into the hall with great fanfare it was a spectacular sight.

SCHNITZ

Many pagan customs of Europe were practiced alongside Christianity with less conflict than one would imagine. Ultimately, the divorce between Christianity and paganism was finalized with the Protestant Reformation. The two could no longer coexist.

Those With Oak Knowledge

Celtic people include the Irish, ancient Britons, and Gauls. There is insufficient evidence to support a theory that ancient Celtic people consciously celebrated the winter solstice or spring equinox. Instead, celebrations are believed to have focused on the opening of the seasons, versus the distance of the sun from the earth.

Most of us have heard about England's Stonehenge, the group of massive stones placed in a mysterious formation, located seemingly in the middle of nowhere. Scholars generally agree that the site was used for religious purposes. A lesser known circular stone formation in Ireland, known as Newgrange, is believed to be at least five thousand years old; older than Stonehenge, and older even than Egypt's pyramids. At dawn on the Winter Solstice, a single shaft of light shines through a crevice at Newgrange's central chamber, lighting up a stone basin beneath carvings of solar discs, eye shapes, and spirals.

CELTIC CROSS

Teutonic and Celtic tribes held feasts in November called "Jiuleis" or "Giuli" for the same reason that feasts were held in Europe: domestic animals had to be killed because they found nothing to eat in frosty pastures. Aerre-geola (before Yule) and Aftera-geola (after Yule), were Anglo Saxon names for December and January. Winter solstice was known as Modranicht or Mother Night. In medieval Ireland, special days were designated to celebrate the changing of the seasons. These days were November 1, February 1, May 1 and August 1. Some of these pagan English festivals are written about in *Ecclesiastical History,* by an eighth century scholar named Bede. Unfortunately, contemporary scholars do not consider his chronicle of pre-Christian practices complete. Because accurate information about pagan practices is disputed, many continue to speculate wildly about long-ago occurrences. It helps to be mindful of this when reading accounts about what "really" happened in ancient pagan cultures.

We know that ancient Celts had a highly ritualized religion headed by Druids, an upper class of priests. At the religion center was the worship of a spectrum of nature gods. Druid ceremonies were held primarily near the source of lakes and rivers in sacred groves of oak trees. The Druids' role was to educate the community's young, as well as recite and preserve the culture's myths, legends, and ballads. Druids were considered society's intellectuals; responsible for tribal history, law, and arbitration. As priests, Druids interpreted omens, presided over rituals, and organized sacrifices. Their knowledge was so vast that priestly training spanned a period of twelve

LEAF COOKIES

to twenty years. They maintained an exclusively oral tradition in order to protect this sacred knowledge. Written records in the wrong hands would be catastrophic to them.

In ancient times, an extensive oak forest covered Europe, providing an ample source of wood supply for fires and homes. Druid came to mean "those with oak knowledge." These trees also offered nutritious sustenance. As early as 4000 BCE, acorns from oaks were ground into flour and baked into bread. Druids most revered oak, but hazel, rowan, and fir trees were considered significant. The holly tree was honored because of its evergreen, winter fruit-bearing properties.

Trees were associated with the four ancient elements: earth, water, air and fire. A tree grows out of the earth, is nourished by water, and its branches spread into air. If struck by lightning, the tree becomes a burning flame. During winter ceremonies, Druids hung apples from branches of oak and fir trees as offerings to

Odin, king of the gods. To honor Balder, the god of light, they placed lighted candles on tree branches.

Parasitic mistletoe commonly grew on apple, poplar and hawthorn trees. Mistletoe thriving on oak trees was considered a sacred symbol of friendship and peace.

Druids noted that although mistletoe was nourished by the tree, it did no harm to it. Each year on the twenty-second of December, a Druid high priest carrying a golden sickle climbed a massive oak. When he located mistletoe, he cut it loose. Below him, attentive priests skillfully caught the plants in their robe skirts because it was considered bad luck for any mistletoe to touch the ground.

MISTLETOE MOBILE

Druids endured until the Christian era. Their traditions held Celtic society together even as invading Romans tried mercilessly to destroy them. Because of their oral font of knowledge, and because history ultimately is written by conquerors, it is difficult to ascertain the truth about who the Druids really were and what they did. The relatively modern Ancient Order of Druids formed in England in 1781 has little to do with the Druids of the Ancient Celts. The Druid name is often used in today's so-called New Age movement, but it has no relation to the original religion.

In 596 CE, Christianity was brought to Anglo-Saxon Great Britain by Saint Augustine and forty of his monks. The Church allowed some traditions to continue but gradually and

NATURE SCAVENGER ORNAMENTS

persistently exchanged the focus of Celtic worship of the Norse god Odin to the worship of Jesus Christ. Anglo-Saxons were reticent to give up their beautiful festival of Yule. The Church realistically acknowledged the challenge it faced to overcome the strong attachment that Celtic people had to their land of huge forests. In 601 CE, the Pope wrote a letter to St. Augustine in England ordering him to decorate Christian churches with greenery, just as pagan temples were decorated with greenery. Only mistletoe was declared unacceptable in these Christian churches because of its reverence by Druids and Celtic people.

Yule logs were popular in England, just as they were in Europe. In both locales, similar protocols directed how to burn and dispose of the log. In the countryside, the Yule log was dragged into the home and greeted by all. Everyone was offered a chance to sit on the log and kiss it. The oldest person would

In parts of Scotland, the first person to open the outside door on Yule would experience good fortune throughout the year because he or she let the Yule into the home. During the holidays, a table was traditionally set and covered with wonderful things to eat and drink so any visitor would find plenty of refreshment during Yule. It was considered rude for any visitor to leave without sampling some goodies.

often pour wine over the log three times and pray for health, prosperity, and the well-being of the home. Spiced ale was enjoyed by all before the log was at last set on fire. It was considered critical for the fire of the old year to last until the beginning of the new year. In some regions, it was thought unwise to give away any light from the fire on the morning of the new year because it could risk taking a family's luck out of the home. On New Year's Eve, a huge public bonfire was lit, followed by much merrymaking.

MINI YULE LOG PLACE FAVORS

The English poet Herrick (1591–1674) beautifully states the requirements of using a piece of last year's Yule log to light the current log, and the importance of saving a piece of the old.

Come, bring witha noise,
My merry, merry boys,
The Christmas Log to the firing;
While my good Dame, she
Bids ye all be free,
And drink to your hearts' desiring.

With the last year's Brand
Light the new Block, and
For good success in his spending,
On your psaltries play,
That sweet luck may
Come while the log is a-teending.

LAMB'S WOOL

Kindle the Christmas brand and then
Til sunset let it burn,
Which, quenched, then lay it up again,
Til Christmas next return.

Part must be kept wherewith to tend,
The Christmas log next year;
And were it safely kept, the fiend
Can do no mischief here.

In many parts of England, an Ashen Faggot was used in place of a Yule log. Several sticks of ash wood were tied together with bands of ash or willow. Often, each of the bands represented daughters in the family. When the first band broke, it signified that the corresponding girl would be first to marry.

Later in England, a Yule log was frequently replaced by an enormous candle. The candle was large enough to burn for the entire day. In the 1700s, chandlers (candle makers) sent their best customers large candles on Christmas Eve, and coopers (barrel makers) sent logs of wood.

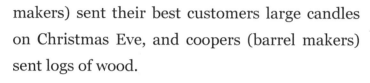

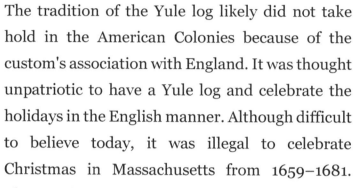

CHOCOLATE YULE LOG

The tradition of the Yule log likely did not take hold in the American Colonies because of the custom's association with England. It was thought unpatriotic to have a Yule log and celebrate the holidays in the English manner. Although difficult to believe today, it was illegal to celebrate Christmas in Massachusetts from 1659–1681. Those who did were fined five shillings, a substantial amount for the times. Historical records document that until at least 1850, Christmas was a day similar to any other—business was conducted, courts were open, and children attended school.

"Wassailing" the fruit trees is another old Celtic and European custom. The term wassail is from the phrase, "Was Haile," a greeting the Saxon lords and ladies called out to each other. It means, "Be of good health." The methods of wassailing vary but the intent is always to bring fertility to orchards, either as an offering to the spirits, or as a devotional rite. The wassail ceremony often began at home where family members dipped hot cakes into cider. Cake and

FRUIT ORNAMENTS

cider were then transported to the orchard where the cake was placed in the crook of a large apple tree branch, and the cider poured over it as an offering.

Alternatively, a farmer and his workers would carry a large jug of cider and head out to the field to circle a tree and drink a toast to it three times. A branch was dipped into the cider. Some of the cider was either sprinkled on the tree or poured over its roots. Sometimes, trunks of trees were beaten and shots were fired through bare branches as part of this boisterous ceremony. Everyone headed to the farmer's house afterward for a feast.

On the Eve of Epiphany in England (January 6), farmers led servants out to a field newly sewn with wheat seeds, then lit thirteen fires, one larger than the rest. The group formed a circle around the fires and drank a cider toast to the anticipated harvest. They later returned to the farmhouse where they consumed cider-soaked caraway seed speckled cakes. On some farms, a large cake with a hole in the middle was placed on the horns of the finest oxen and all drank toasts to the oxen on the farm.

Another British agricultural ritual was the custom of "burning the bush." A ball of branches from a hawthorn tree was positioned in a farmhouse kitchen and left to hang there all year. On New Year's Day, it was relocated to a wheat field where it was tossed into a large fire of straw and bushes. While it burned, a new bundle of hawthorn was made, and the ends of its branches were scorched in the fire. Some burning straw from the fire was carried over twelve ridges of the farmer's

Wassailing Toasts

Wassail the Trees that they my beare
You many a Plum and many a Peare;
For more or lesse fruits they will bring,
As you do give them Wassailing.

Apples and pears, with right good corn
Come in plenty to everyone;
Eat and drink good cake and hot ale,
Give Earth to drink, and she'll not fail.

Here's to thee, old apple tree,
Whence thou may'st bud and whence though may'st blow!
And whence thou may'st bear apples enow!
Hats full! Caps full!
Bushel-bushel sacks full!
And my pockets full too! Huzza!

fields. All of this was followed by cheers, celebration, and lots of hard cider, a fermented alcoholic brew.

CELTIC CROSS BREAD

On December twenty-first, poor English women traveled door-to-door collecting gifts of wheat or flour so they could make Christmas bread and cake for their families. In return, the wealthier women would receive a piece of mistletoe or holly, believed to bring good luck to the generous household. This practice was known as "Thomassing," or "curning." Households often donated up to a quart of flour. When several stops were made, this contribution represented an important addition to a poor family's larder.

During winter holidays, crowds of merrymakers dressed in costumes filled the streets. Guising, also known as mumming, was popular in the British Isles, France, and southern and eastern Europe during the Middle Ages. Guising is related to the word disguise but the origin of the word mumming is not clear. The custom is thought to have come from the Roman Saturnalia.

MUMMER'S MASK

The most popular costume was an animal head. There was also considerable cross-dressing between genders. In later years, clothes were turned inside out and strips of torn cloth were sewn onto them. Mummers often wore headdresses featuring dangling ribbons to cover faces. A face was often blackened to ensure anonymity and increase fantasy. Mummers sang, danced, and begged door to door, conducting plays for anyone who would watch. The plays featured stock characters portraying the ancient saga of the death of the old year and the birth of the new. Audiences watched two actor antagonists fight to a mock death, at which time the noble actor would be revived as a hero. The exact age of the mummer's play tradition is unknown, but some believe it predates the Roman era. Not surprisingly, the Church disapproved of the revelry and abandon that characterized mumming. Common people continued to enjoy the festivities despite their conflict with the observance of a Christian holiday.

During pagan times, a horse was often sacrificed to Woden at the Yule season. Over time, this evolved into the interesting English and European custom where a mock horse pranced up to houses on holiday nights. The mock horse was constructed by using a real horse's skull or a wooden carving of a horse's head. An attached cloth covered a group of young men functioning together as the body. The horse would beg for treats for its human attendants, scaring children along the way. In Wales, this horse was called the Mari Llwyd. In Germany, it was the Schimmel (gray horse). In England, it was known as the Old Hob, giving birth to the term hobby horse.

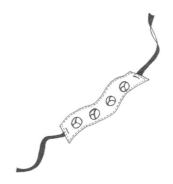

JINGLE BELL BAND

In Yorkshire, England, "frumenty" was the first food consumed on Christmas morning. The name comes from the Latin word, frumentum, meaning corn, although there is no corn in the dish. The practice of serving "frumenty" may have originated from a cereal sacrament intended to embody the power of corn. "Frumenty" was made of hulled wheat cooked in milk, then sweetened with cinnamon and sugar. A similar Scottish grain dish was served early on Christmas morning to family members who were still in bed. This dish, called "new sowens," was made of husks and siftings of oatmeal, cooked to the consistency of molasses.

Prior to the Roman, Angles and Saxons influence, the Celtic god named Dagda perpetually stirred a huge caldron called "undry" in the British Isles. Undry was filled with a porridge made of cereal, fruits, and meats—a mixture representing the bounty of the earth. Celtic people served this dish of the gods at their feasts.

Another Medieval celebration called the "Feast of Fools" was popular in England and Europe. It featured parallels to the Roman Saturnalia and remnants of a much earlier time in history. This festival took place within the confines of the church where upper-level clergy would change roles with their subordinates. One participant was elected to be a mock bishop or mock pope called the Lord of Misrule. In Scotland, this person was known as the Abbot of Unreason. The Lord of Misrule would take his "court" of fellow revelers through the church and create a bawdy parody out of its rituals and the institution in general. Many rules of social order were turned upside down. Flamboyant costumes and cross-dressers were a common sight. Participants played riotous music, danced in pews, rode hobby horses down aisles, and set off firecrackers under the pulpit. The festivities eventually spilled out into the streets, where town residents joined in the merrymaking. The crowd added energy with lively music, parades, and increasingly more risqué parody. The festival took on a life of its own. It was finally suppressed in the late sixteenth century.

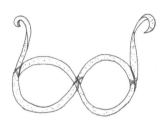

ORANGE PEEL SPECTACLES

Gather acorns outside before the first snow. At your winter solstice fire, throw acorns into the flames one at a time, giving thanks for the old year and remembering all that was good.

Christmas trees were not a common sight in England until 1847. Although Henry VIII had a gold tree at Christmas in 1516, and Queen Charlotte had a tree in the 1800s, the common people did not yearn for trees themselves. When Queen Victoria married her German cousin Albert in 1840, Albert brought the customs of his country with him. Until that time, holiday presents were placed in stockings hung by the chimney.

"Boxing Day" is another Celtic holiday held in England on the day after Christmas. The concept can be traced back to Roman times when money was collected in little clay boxes, then given to servants making deliveries. On the twenty-sixth of December, English village priests opened the "poor box" in which they had collected alms during the year, and distributed its contents to those in need. This evolved into a practice of giving Christmas boxes to household servants and also those who provided public service. Eventually, brazen opportunists approached the wealthy, hoping to benefit from some Boxing Day generosity. Many people on the giving side of this custom came to see this practice as a burden.

After Boxing Day, the festivities continued, incorporating many interesting ways to celebrate New Year's Day and other holidays culminating the season. According to custom, only gifts related to the celebration of the new year were to be given away on New Year's day. If other items were given or even loaned, bad luck in the new year could occur. It was considered important to keep the balance in favor of receiving, rather than giving or paying out, in order to positively affect this outcome.

APPLE PLACE SETTING

In Scotland, Christmas is more of a quiet, religious occasion. New Year festivities called Hogmanay are the time for excess energy to be released. Although the origin of the word Hogmanay is disputed, it may have derived from the cheese and oatcake offerings given to groups of children who traveled the streets. Covered by long sheets, they resembled Chinese dragons. They made their way through villages, singing:

"Get up goodwife, and shake your feathers,

And dinna think that we are beggars;

For we are bairns come out to play,

Get up and gie's our hogmanay."

Another Scottish custom is called the "First Footer." The first visitor of the new year is thought to bring good luck. The First Footer brings magical gifts representing wishes for the new year: a piece of coal for warmth, a piece of bread for food, and money or salt for wealth. This song was sung at doorways on New Year's Eve on the Isle of Man located in the Irish Sea.

SEASONS BREAD

Again we assemble, a merry New Year
To wish to each one of the family here,
Whether man, woman, or girl, or boy,
That long life and happiness all may enjoy;
May they of potatoes and herrings have plenty,
With butter and cheese, and each other dainty;
And may their sleep never, by night or by day,
Disturbed be by even the tooth of a flea;
Until at the Quaaltagh again we appear,
To wish you, as now, all a happy New Year.

At midnight on New Year's Eve, it was customary to open all windows for a few minutes to let bad luck out, and allow good luck in. On New Year's Day, it was considered unwise to wash household linen or sweep floors for fear that the luck of the house could be washed or swept away.

WHEEL OF THE YEAR WREATH

Another holiday, held nearly two weeks after Boxing Day, was "Plough Monday." Occurring the first Monday after Twelfth Day (January 6), it marked the end of the holidays and the time for regular work to resume. On this day, young men from local farms hung ribbons from their clothes, then yoked themselves to a plow. A small band of musicians led the way while the young men pulled the plow from house to house, attempting to collect money. A "fool" accompanying them carried an inflated bladder tied to the end of a long stick with which he whipped the "oxen" pulling the plow. When money was offered, the young men shouted "Largess!" (A gift well given!), then performed a dance around the plow. If money was requested but not received, the team would likely plow some of the homeowner's land that was not normally meant to be disturbed.

Also occurring after Epiphany was St. Distaff's, or Rock Day. Rock Day derives from "rocken," the German word for distaff. A distaff is a stick for holding wool or flax while spinning. On this day, women would resume duties of spinning after the long holiday season. To add merrymaking to the occasion, men pretended to burn the women's flax, and as a counter measure, women poured water over the men.

What About Santa Claus?

Berchta, Teutonic pagan goddess of winter and domestic arts, is also known as the protector of children. During cold and dark nights at the end of the year, Berchta rides over the countryside in a wagon, or on a light colored horse, or sometimes accompanied by a goose—an image later associated with Mother Goose. Berchta stops at each home, enters through the chimney, then leaves tokens for well-behaved children, or lumps of coal for those who have misbehaved. At every house, she expects to find food available. If conditions are unsatisfactory, a curse on the household is risked. The Church disapproved of Berchta's strong pagan roots. Over time, her benevolent persona transformed into that of a disreputable shrewish old woman or witch. As Berchta's favor faded, a replacement for a protector of children was sought.

WINDOW COOKIE

Enter, Santa Claus!

His character is an amalgam of colorful figures of world mythology, all synonymous with the concept of unselfish giving.

Denmark: Jule-nissen, Sankt Nikolaus, Sint Nicolaas, Santa Klaas
England: Father Christmas
France: Petit Jesus, Pere Noel, Tante Aria
Italy: Befana, Babbo Natale
Germany: Kriss Kringle, Krist Kindlein, Weihnachtsman
Russia: Baboushka, Father Ice, Grandfather Frost
Desert Lands: The Gentle Camel
Czechoslovakia: Svaty Mikulas
Holland: Sinterklaas

Norse believed winter began when "The Old Man of Winter" drove his herds of reindeer south. He was also known as Winter Man, King Frost, King Yule, Old Winter, Grandfather Frost, and Father Christmas.

> Santa Claus has a diverse derivative lineage.
>
> Saturn Roman god of agriculture
>
> Cronos Greek god who became known as Father Time
>
> Holly King Celtic god of the dying year
>
> Thor Norse sky god who sits in a chariot drawn by goats
>
> Odin Scandinavian/Teutonic god known as All Father
>
> Frey Norse god of fertility
>
> Tomte Norse spirit of the land who gave gifts to children

Folktale expert Clement Moore, author of the poem, "Twas the Night Before Christmas," chose eight reindeer for Saint Nicholas as homage to Sleipner, Odin's eight legged horse from Norse mythology. Reindeer have also been associated with Herne, the horned god of the Celts.

The Santa Claus we know today is a rotund man with rosy cheeks and a happy smile. This version is derived from a 1931 painting by artist Haddon Sundblom. When commissioned by Coca-Cola to render an image of Santa for an advertisement, Sundblom used as a model his Muskegon, Michigan neighbor, salesman Lou Prentis.

Science

On or around the twenty-second of December, the sun appears at the lowest point in the sky because the Earth is farthest from the sun. This marks the shortest day of the year and the longest night—the true beginning of winter. As the Earth continues its elliptical track around the opposite side of the Sun, the northern hemisphere heads toward spring and days lengthen almost imperceptibly. The southern hemisphere heads toward winter.

At one time, Europe celebrated the new year on the twenty-first of March—the Vernal Equinox—the first full moon of spring. Peasants who resisted changing the beginning of the new year to January were called April Fools.

The Roman Julian calendar originally consisted of three-hundred-sixty-five days and six hours. Calendar planners had not considered the discrepancy between the lengths of solar and lunar years. By the sixteenth century, this inaccurate calibration set the vernal equinox on the eleventh of March instead of the twenty-first of March. Too many extra days had accumulated over the years to keep things straight. During the 1500s, Pope Gregory XIII and his Italian astronomers rectified this. His team subtracted ten days from the calendar to correct course, then developed a plan to systematically add leap days. In 1582, December was changed from the tenth month of the year to the twelfth. The new calendar became known as the Gregorian calendar. Resistance to the Pope's ruling stemmed from the belief that precious days had been stolen from people's lives. The Gregorian calendar was not used by England and Colonial America until the 1700s

Music

The word carol describes a pre Christian circle or sun dance accompanied by singing. The origin of the word is uncertain but the related Latin word "carolare" means to sing. The Greek word "choraulein" describes a dance where a chorus and flute provide music. Choros means dance; urlein means to play the flute. From it are derived the words choir and choral.

In ancient religious ceremonies, people often held hands as they danced in circles and sang. They moved in a circular pattern during the stanzas, then marched in place during the chorus. In twelfth century France, a carol was a dance song sung to herald the coming of spring. In Italy, it was sung as accompaniment to a ring dance. In Russia, ancient pagan songs were called "Kolyada." In England, carols were often singing and dancing with no relation to religion.

"The Holly and the Ivy," is an ancient carol probably originating in France. It contains the remnants of Nature worship of a pre-Christian era. The song describes the battle for power between the male (holly) and female (ivy) plants, and was likely sung while pagan boys and girls danced.

The first Christmas hymns sung in memory of the birth of Jesus were unpopular among peasants because they were sung in Latin, a language understood only by priests. Most Christian carols derived from slowed dance songs. Familiar tunes with new words helped instruct pagan people in Christian ways but the original dances and songs were ultimately banned by the Church because of their sensual nature.

Bells were used to announce happy and sad events long before the spread of Christianity. In Egypt they were rung at the feast of Osiris. Jewish high priests wore robes adorned with bells. They used hand bells during ceremonies. Ancient Greeks priests used bells in ceremonies, too. Emperor Augustus hung a bell in front of the temple of Jupiter.

At dawn on New Year's Day in South Wales, poor children carried a jug of fresh well water through their village. They dipped a sprig of evergreen into the water then sprinkled those they met, spreading best wishes for a happy holiday season. This carol was sung for those who were inside or asleep and missed the sprinkling:

"Here we bring new water
From the well so clear,
For to worship god with
This happy New Year.
Sing levy-dew, sing levy-dew,
The water and the wine;
The seven bright gold wires
And the bugles they do shine.
Sing reign of Fair Maide,
With gold upon her toe,--
Open you the West door,
And turn the Old Year go:
Sing reign of Fair Maid,
With gold upon her chin,--
Open you the East door,
And let the New Year in."

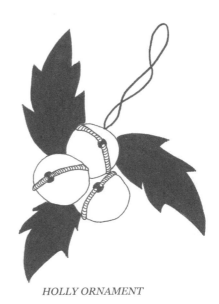

HOLLY ORNAMENT

CRAFTS

Egypt/Mesopotamia

Mother Pot

Nature is often referred to as Mother Nature. The ancient symbol for mother is the water pot or vase.

Find a pot that complements your table and fill it with water.

Arrange greenery around it and display as a reminder of the deep and fertile womb of nature.

This is also a nice way to hydrate a room against the dry heat of winter.

Miphletzeth (or Mipleceth)

This oval figure is an emblem of Asherah, the Canaanite mother goddess. It represents the doorway where life enters the world. A symbol of both fertility and wealth, its counterpart is the thyrsus of Dionysus or the rod of Hermes.

If you are lucky enough to find a small, smooth stone with a hole in it, use it!

NEED

Self-hardening modeling clay or bakeable molding compound

Baking tray

A length of black silk cord, long enough to fit the special person who will wear the miphletzeth

MAKE

Shape clay into oval.

Use damp hands to smooth bumps or cracks.

Poke hole through top of oval, large enough to thread cord.

Transfer to baking tray.

Allow to harden overnight, or bake according to instructions.

Thread cord. Wear as pendant or hang as decoration.

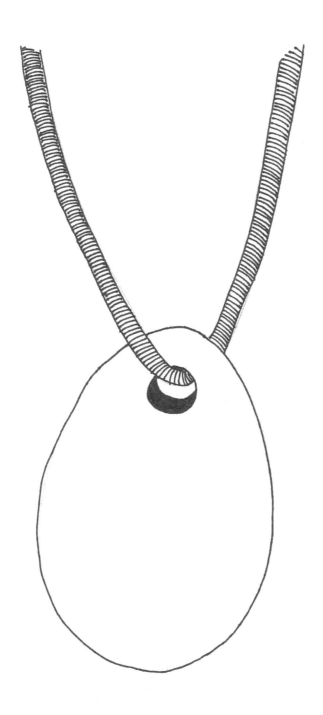

MIPHLETZETH

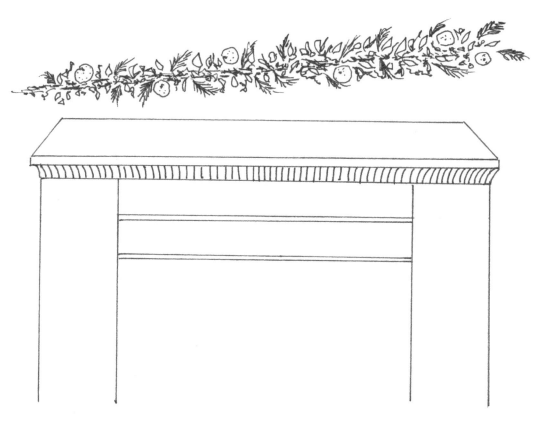

RHAMNA

Greek

Rhamna

On Christmas morning on the Island of Chios in Greece, tenants offer landlords wooden poles entwined with myrtle, olive, and orange leaves. This delightful display is called a rhamna. Geraniums and anemones are added to it, as well as oranges, lemons and strips of gold colored paper.

Construct this fragrant and attractive arrangement as a gift to give during holiday visits. It looks especially nice hanging horizontally over a fireplace mantle.

NEED

One slender but sturdy branch, 3' long

Myrtle, olive, and orange leaves (from a florist)

Fresh flowers

A few fresh oranges and lemons

Gold colored ribbon, cut into 24" segments

Floral wire

MAKE

Cut large shoots off branch.

Attach greenery to branch with floral wire.

Cut long twists of lemon and orange peels. Wind twists around branch.

Attach gold ribbon streamers onto branch.

Attach flowers onto branch at pleasing intervals, using floral wire.

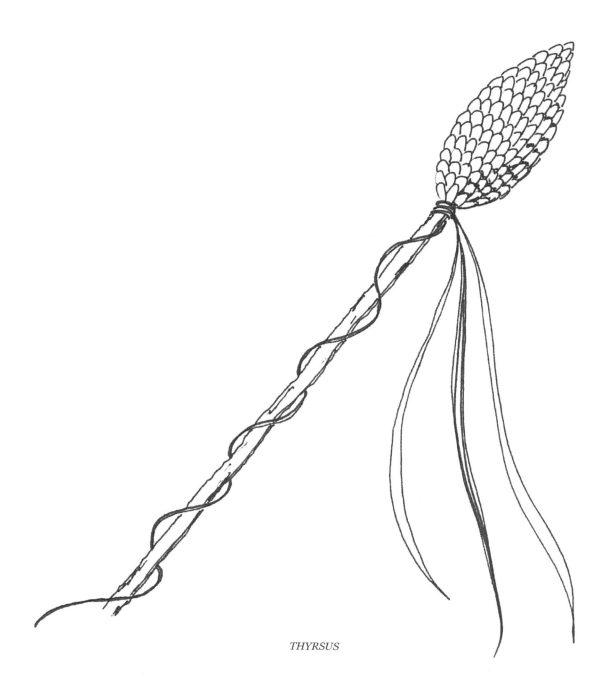

THYRSUS

Thyrsus

The Thyrsus is a pine torch used as part of the Festival of Dionysus, Greek god of wine and fertility. His fifth of January celebration marked a shift away from adoration of an earth mother, paving the way for Christianity. In evening rituals to honor Dionysus and the evergreen, pine torches were carried by each person to light the ceremonies. The Thyrsus is a totem of fertility, life, and revivification, as well as drunkenness and revelry. The wand is also a phallic symbol. We are reminded of that connection today when we see old fashioned bed posts topped with pinecones.

NEED

One large pinecone

One sturdy twig, 3' long

Cloth ribbons in various textures and colors

Ivy or vine leaf garland (optional)

One flat twig or craft stick

Floral wire or twine

MAKE

Peel petals approximately 1" off pinecone base.

Using flat twig as a splint to strengthen attachment between pinecone and large stick, tie twine around large stick and pinecone base, sandwiching the flat twig between both to make a sturdy connection.

Attach ribbons, ivy, or vine leaves to pinecone base and around twig.

Group several thyrsus together in a vase and position on floor in a cozy corner. Hang another thyrsus over a door frame.

Roman

Janus Coins

January is a magical time of year when past meets present. On these two-faced coins, Roman god Janus looks both ahead and behind, seeing past and future. Hang these coins from your dining room chandelier or fireplace garland.

NEED

Copper colored self-hardening modeling clay or bakeable molding compound

Ribbon for hanging

Small drinking glass to form and cut clay shape

Rolling pin

Glue

Baking tray

MAKE

Roll clay to ¼" thick. Use drinking glass to cut clay into circles.

Carefully remove excess clay from circle edge.

Use damp hands to smooth bumps or cracks.

Transfer circles to baking tray.

With toothpick, etch design for Janus's face onto circle.

Poke hole into top of circle for threading ribbon.

Allow clay circles to harden overnight, or bake according to instructions.

Apply glue to blank sides of two circles, then press together, matching pre-punctured holes. Allow to dry. Thread ribbon through hole and hang.

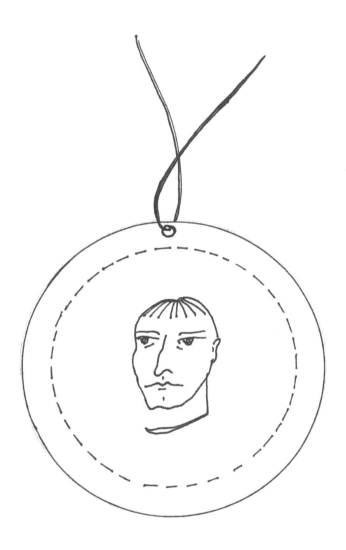

JANUS COIN

Knitted Pileus Cap

In Roman times, these hats signified freedom from slavery. During the Saturnalia, slaves and masters exchanged places. This rolled brim hat looks similar to the felted pileus cap worn by freed slaves. Pattern is for adult sizes small (20"), medium (21.5"), and large (22.5"). To create a felt cap, knit large size with 100% wool, wash finished cap in hot water, then dry on high. Repeat to shrink further.

NEED

1 skein worsted weight yarn

Circular needles, size 6, 16" long

Marker

MAKE

Cast on 90 (96, 102) stitches. Join ends and work one round. Place marker.

Knit every round for 6 inches in Stockinette stitch.

Begin decrease, repeating pattern from *

Round 1: *Knit 13 (14, 15) Knit 2 together (repeat from *) 84 (90, 96 stitches)

Round 2: Knit

Round 3: *Knit 12 (13,14) Knit 2 together (repeat from *) 78 (84,90 stitches)

Round 4: Knit

Round 5: *Knit 11 (12,13) Knit 2 together (repeat from *) 72 (78, 84 stitches)

Round 6: Knit

Continue Round 5 pattern until 48 stitches remain.

Decrease every round until 6 stitches remain.

Cut yarn and draw through last stitch to fasten.

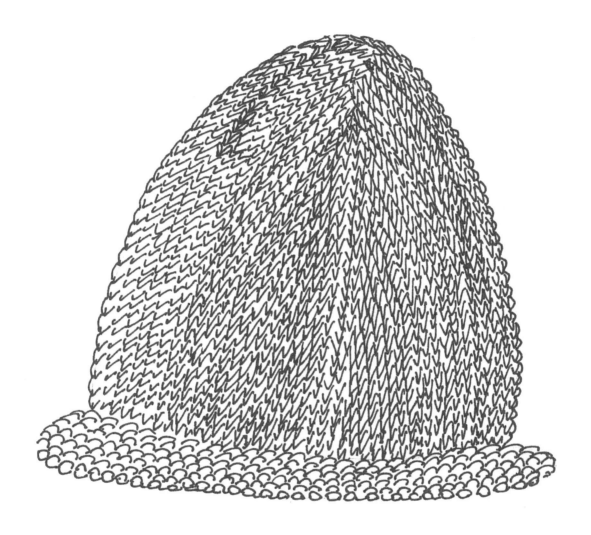

KNITTED PILEUS CAP

Sigillaria

During holidays, Romans exchanged little clay dolls in shapes resembling animals and humans. These are both ancestors of holiday greeting cards and likely vestiges of the ancient practice of sacrifice.

NEED

Self-hardening modeling clay or bakeable molding compound

Cardboard for stencils

Rolling pin

Baking tray

Clear polyurethane spray, or colored paints

Ribbon for hanging

MAKE

Trace templates onto cardboard. Cut shapes. Or, design your own sheep, cows, ducks, etc.

Roll out clay to ¼" thick.

Using cardboard stencils, trace shapes onto clay.

Transfer shapes to baking tray.

Use damp hands to smooth bumps or cracks.

Make hole on top of each figure to thread ribbon.

Allow to harden overnight, or bake according to instructions.

Paint sigillaria as desired, or coat with clear polyurethane to make shiny.

Allow to dry. Thread ribbon through hole.

Wear as necklace, hang from ceiling, or use as tree ornament.

SIGILLARIA

Luminaries

In Roman times, lanterns were given as gifts to encourage light and warmth in the coming year. Add a warm glow to a snowy walkway outside your home on a cold winter night.

NEED

Small paper bags (plain or colored)

Colored tissue paper

Tea candles or votive candles

Sand, dirt, or pebbles

Tape or glue

MAKE

Draw simple designs on side of paper bag. Laurel wreaths and the winged figure of Mercury are traditional, but trees, suns, and moons are fun, too.

Cut designs out of bag.

Measure a piece of colored tissue paper to span the bag design.

Tape or glue it onto inside of bag.

Add sand, dirt, or pebbles to bottom of bag to prevent tipping.

Place tea or votive candle into bag.

Light candle and enjoy the glow.

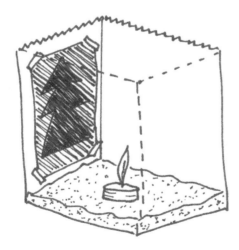

LUMINARIES

Masks

Animal masks were especially popular during the Roman Saturnalia. Creating masks and costumes today can counter the focus on seasonal consumerism. Use empty boxes and excess wrapping matter for material.

Papier Mache Mask

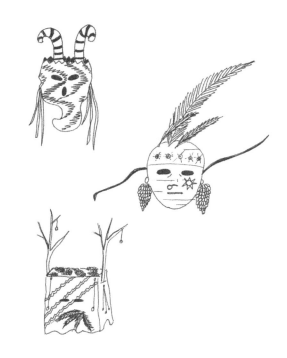

NEED

Cardboard, poster board, and stiff corrugated cardboard

Newspaper, cut or torn into strips, 1" x 12"

Stapler and staples

Wide dish or pan

Flour

Balloon to provide frame for mask during construction

Decorations for mask can include paint, yarn, feathers, beads, tissue paper, fake jewels, string, colored thread, pipe cleaners, dried flowers, pinecones.

MAKE

Create and draw mask concept.

Measure two 3" wide strips of cardboard long enough to fit around masquerader's head. Add additional 2" to length to accommodate overlap. Cut.

Glue strips together, one over the other, to increase stability.

Check sizing. Staple headband ends together.

Place headband on surface. Stuff with crumpled paper to maintain shape while glue dries.

If antlers or horns are desired, cut shapes from corrugated cardboard, then attach to headband, using stapler. Paint these appendages later or use as base for further elaboration.

In wide pot, prepare paper mache mixture. Gradually stir together ¼ cup flour and 4 cups water. Boil and stir mixture until smooth and creamy. Let cool.

Remove crumbled newspaper from inside double-thick cardboard headband.

Inflate balloon to approximate size of head, then position cardboard band around it. This will provide a frame over which to apply paper mache as you build the mask. (Balloon will be popped once mask is dry.)

Dip a few strips at a time into cooled paste mixture. Remove excess paste from each strip by running strip through fingers. Begin layering individual pieces over headband and over front of balloon.

Continue layering strips vertically and horizontally, using crisscross pattern to increase stability. Evenly distribute strips so no section is thicker than another. Leave slits open for eyes.

When mask is complete, prop upright so nothing touches wet sections. Set aside.

Allow to dry several days. Once mask is thoroughly dry, pop balloon.

Paint mask as desired. Use glue gun to attach embellishments.

Plaster Gauze Mask

This mask is best for adults and teenagers. Young children may not tolerate this facial cast process. Purchase ready-made plaster masks with generic expressions for them.

NEED

Plaster gauze roll

Baby oil or petroleum jelly

Scissors

Clean rag

Newspaper

Awl

Ribbon, used to tie finished mask to head, 1 ½" x 36"

Embellishments such as feathers, jewels, ribbons, and paint

MAKE

Unroll gauze and cut multiple strip lengths; 2", 4", and 6".

Soak gauze in water according to package directions.

Pull subject's hair off face and position subject face-up over clean rag on floor. Subject must agree to maintain a relaxed expression during mask-making process. Smear oil or petroleum jelly onto subject's face, especially on eyebrows and wherever gauze will be applied.

Remove one 2" strip gauze from water. Slide gauze between fingers to remove excess plaster.

Holding side of strip with more plaster away from subject's skin, place first layer on forehead. Continue layering 2" strips, leaving openings for eyes, nose, and mouth. Develop crosswise pattern to create smooth and strong surface. Apply gauze only over areas completely covered by oil or petroleum jelly.

Continue process, graduating to 4" strips after 2" strip supply is depleted, until face is covered. Repeat, forming second layer. Let set till firm, but not dry.

Apply third layer with 4" strips only, continuing smooth and uniform pattern to create an optimal finished product. Tuck end edges under where possible.

Let mask set on face for approximately 15 minutes, taking care to engage with subject to diminish claustrophobic sensation.

After 15 minutes, instruct subject to make various expressions to break seal and release mask from skin.

Once separated, carefully lift mask off face without bending it.

Mark position above eye slits on mask sides where ribbon holding mask will connect. Use awl to puncture holes.

Place on newspaper. Allow to dry overnight or longer.

To decorate, paint mask surface or leave as is. Use glue gun to attach embellishments.

Paper Bag Mask

NEED

One plain brown paper grocery bag

Scissors

Masking tape

Glue

Embellishments: markers, ribbons, construction paper, paint, feathers, sticks, and yarn, etc.

MAKE

To fit and rest bag on shoulders, cut "U" shapes at open sides. Reinforce inside of cut areas with masking tape. Reserve cut matter for embellishment material.

Mark position of eyes on bag. Draw creative eye designs, then cut holes for pupils.

Make ear shapes and glue onto sides of bag. Hang earrings.

Glue antlers, horns, or hair to top or sides of mask.

Glue folded triangle shape to nose area.

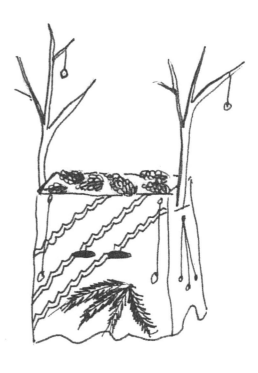

Greeting

Frame and hang the traditional Roman seasonal greeting in a prominent place. "Anno novo faustum felix tibi sit" translation: "May the new year be happy and lucky for you."

NEED

Heavy paper

Thick marker

Photo frame

Twigs or fir sprigs

Glue

MAKE

Copy quote in pencil, then darken with marker.

Place inside wooden frame.

Glue twigs or pine sprigs to frame corners.

Allow to dry. Hang.

Boxes

Romans presented gifts of money in little boxes. A small handmade box adds a personal touch to any offering.

NEED

2 sheets of paper, sturdy but foldable, for box top and bottom

1 sheet of thicker contrast color paper to line inside box bottom

Scissors

MAKE

Cut first sheet of paper into precise square shape for box top. Decorate one side of this sheet. Cut second sheet of paper into precise square shape, 1/8" smaller than first.for box bottom. Decorate one side of this sheet.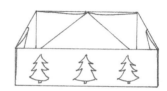

Lay larger first square flat on table, plain side facing up. Fold paper in half horizontally. Open. Fold outside edges to middle fold. Open. Fold paper in half vertically, plain side still facing up. Open. Fold outside edges to middle fold. Do not open.

Fold each outer corner to meet each first horizontal fold. Glue down triangle folds. Allow to dry.

For box top, carefully separate vertical center fold, adjusting triangle ends until box shape appears. Repeat process with second sheet of paper for box bottom. Glue down exterior triangles of both box bottom and top.

For box lining, lay sheet of thicker contrast color paper on table. Place box bottom on it and trace outside with pencil. Cut contrast color paper slightly inside pencil outline. Insert into bottom of box. Adjust size, if needed. Place box top over box bottom. Wrap ribbon twice around box. Top with tiny pine cone or fir sprig.

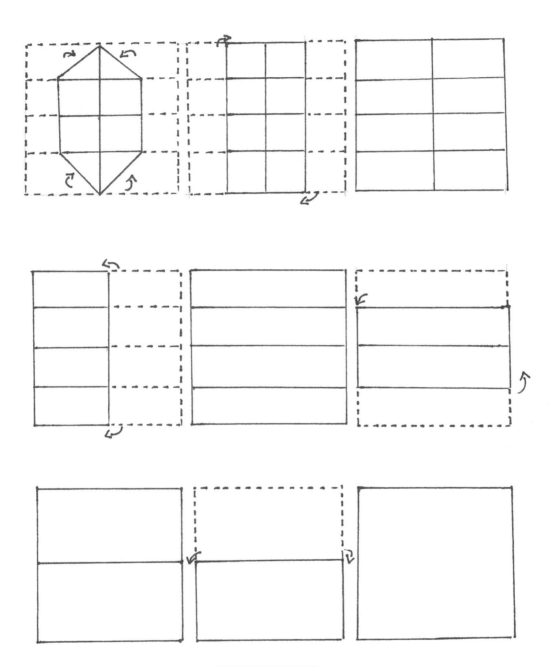

BOX INSTRUCTIONS

Norse

Julbok (or Julbuk)

The Julbok, a Norse goat decoration made of straw, is one of the variety of straw animals called "Jul-docka." The Julbok represents the sacred goat of Thor, Norse god of thunder. Straw was used to make the goat because it was symbolic of grain, and therefore, food and prosperity. During religious ceremonies, a man dressed in a goatskin and goat mask carried the Julbok. This practice was later banned by both Catholic and Protestant churches who considered the goat an alias of Satan.

NEED

Straw from local feed store; bendable wire; red ribbon; scissors

MAKE

Trim rough ends from straw stalks. Soak stalks in bathtub, overnight. Drain, and lay straw on towel. Separate two large sections for inner and outer Julbok body, two smaller bunches for legs, another small bunch for antlers, and one more for the face. Bend section designated for inside of body into a "U" shape. Secure rough ends together with wire.

Bend four equally long bunches separately to fold over opposite sides of the body "U" shape to form legs. Secure underneath body and at leg knee area. Fold second large body section into "U" and wrap around body base, leaving longer loop end to form neck. Cover legs and length of body with remainder. Secure midsection with wire. At opposite end, fold tail section inward, then upward, to form perky tail.

Feed small straw bunch through loop at neck, then point it upward to form antlers. Feed another bunch through loop below antlers to form face. Secure both with wire. Braid antlers, or wind wire around each stalk. Tie red ribbon around face, neck, antlers and body. Trim all ends so Julbok can stand.

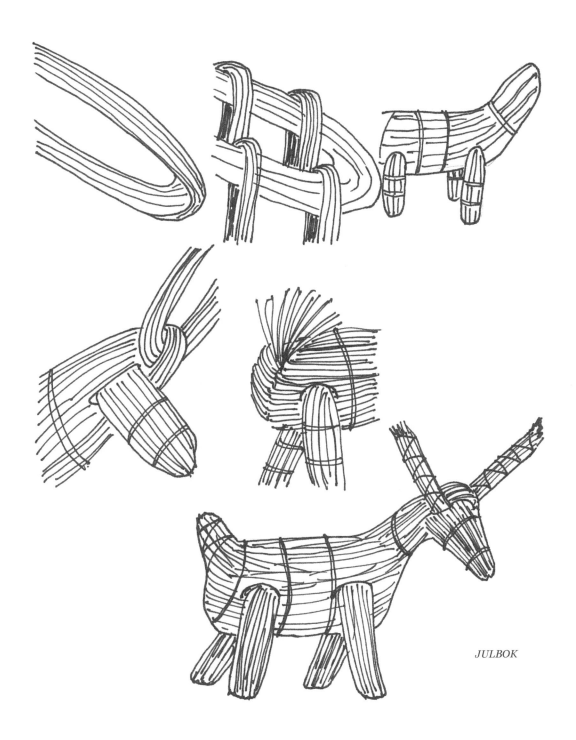

JULBOK

Julenek or Yule Tree Ornaments

Inviting nature inside was popular in Norway. Farm families spread fresh hay on bedroom floors before retiring for the night. Upon waking, the straw was scattered across fields to encourage a good harvest.

Make simple inexpensive representations of nature for your home. Gather material in the fall before snow covers the grass.

NEED

Several clumps of long, dry grass

Several small twigs

Satin ribbon

Clear nylon thread

MAKE

Use a piece of ribbon to tie together
a clump of dried grass and a twig.

Attach a loop of clear nylon thread.

Hang on tree.

St. Lucia Day or Little Yule Costumes

According to the old calendar, Little Yule or Saint Lucia's Day was the shortest day of the year. The oldest or youngest daughter in the family traditionally has the honor of wearing the candle headdress and carrying the tray of food to household members on this special morning. Other daughters may wear coronets of silver tinsel and sons may wear cone hats. Make matching white robes by folding in half a piece of white material, cutting a slit for the neck, and adding a red ribbon around the waist.

Silver Garland Coronet

NEED

Silver garland, long enough to fit around head, with additional 4" overlap

Red satin ribbon, 2" x 5'

Floral wire

MAKE

Wind garland around head for accurate fit.

Attach ends with floral wire.

Tie ribbon into bow.

Attach to crown.

Candle crown

No need to use real candles when practical and safe battery powered candles can be purchased at craft stores or online. Cover the battery base with greenery.

NEED

Ready-made wreath base purchased at craft store

Evergreen boughs, ivy, or other greens

Floral wire

9 battery-powered candles

Red satin ribbon, 2" x 5'

Brown or green felt, 2" x 24"

Glue

MAKE

Fold felt piece in half lengthwise. Trim length to fit inside wreath. Glue to wreath.

Using floral wire, attach candles at uniform intervals around outside of crown.

Add greens to wreath, covering candle bases.

Wind floral wire securely around boughs and shoots to create groomed look.

Tie ribbon into bow, leaving long streamers. Attach to back of crown.

CANDLE CROWN

Cone Hat

On St. Lucia Day or Luciadagen, boys wear cone hats. These can be made of heavy water color paper, poster board, or extremely stiff cloth.

NEED

One poster board

Stapler and staples

String and pencil

Ribbon, ¾" by 48"

Tape

MAKE

With poster board on flat surface, locate center top edge. Mark with pencil.

Tie 36" string to pencil.

To create cone shape, hold string end onto mark with one hand and use other hand to hold pencil securely. Pull string taut. Draw big arc across poster board.

Cut off excess paper surrounding arc.

Matching right and left lower corners, overlap to form cone, fit hat to head. Staple together. Trim.

Cut 48" ribbon in half.

Mark ribbon placement ½" from hat bottom edge.

Cut ¾" horizontal slits for ribbon where indicated. Use tape to reinforce slits. Thread ribbon through slit and pull ends until they meet. Tie together.

For variation, cover finished hat with foil. Tuck under loose ends. Cut paper or white felt stars and glue onto hat.

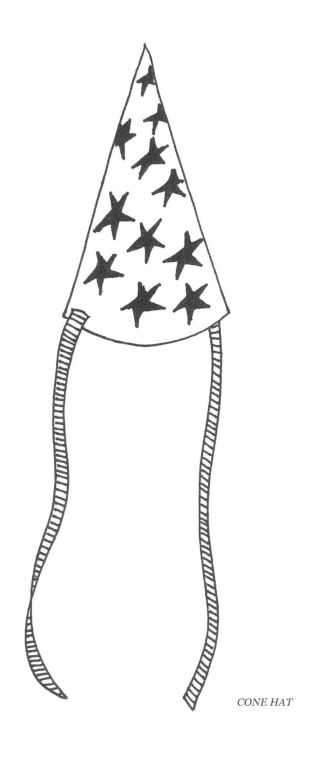

CONE HAT

GIFT WRAPPING

Gift Wrapping

Norse traditionally wrap with white paper, red twine, and red sealing wax. A note with a rhyme containing a clue is attached to the contents of the package.

Gift Tags

NEED

Poster board

Markers

Red twine

Red sealing wax

Sealing wax stamp

MAKE

Cut poster board into rectangle; 3" x 5".

Compose and write rhyme on upper third of rectangle. Fold over one third.

Punch a hole or make a slit in folded corner. Thread twine or ribbon through card.

Seal edge with sealing wax.

Wrapping Paper

NEED

Newsprint

Markers, crayons, paint, glitter

MAKE

Place paper on floor a few layers thick to reduce chance of ripping during decorating. Use plain paper layers as cushion/lining when wrapping.

Trace hands or feet of family members onto paper. Color or embellish.

European

Wreath Making

"Wraeth," Anglo Saxon for wreath, means twisted band. Representing eternal life, wreaths have been found in pharaohs' tombs in Egypt.

Balsam is the most commonly used evergreen for wreaths in the Northeast. Pine is another good option. Spruce and hemlock are poor choices because their needles are not long-lived. Mixing a variety of greens with herbs on a wreath creates an interesting effect. When harvesting greens, draw from trees growing in moist areas. Needles of well hydrated trees tend to stay on their branches longer. Gather pine cones to add to the wreath. When stored outside in cool air, wreaths will often last a few months.

NEED

A wire wreath ring

Floral wire; garden clippers; gloves

Assorted greens, pine cones, and optional bow

MAKE

Lay wreath ring on flat surface.

Lace first bough over wreath ring. Wind wire around both.

Turn wreath over. Repeat process, laying bough on ring and winding wire around both. Flip again. Add another bough, one inch from first, facing same direction.

Continue this flip and add process around ring circumference.

While tying boughs, add pinecones or berries.

Fasten bow with florist wire. Attach wire loop to back of wire frame.

Hang wreath. Mist daily.

WREATH MAKING

Pine Cone Wreath

A pine cone wreath is a reminder of the festival of Dionysius.

NEED

One wire cone wreath ring, usually with three ring levels

Pine cones

Assorted nuts

Flexible wire

Garden clippers, needle nose pliers

MAKE

Harvest pine cones, most uniformly large, some very small for filler. Store this supply outdoors, or dampen pinecones with water several hours before assembling, to close petals and facilitate tighter arrangement.

Place wreath ring on surface.

One pinecone at a time, wind wire under petals, then attach pinecone to wreath's innermost ring, with cones pointing away from center, perpendicular to ring wires. Repeat around ring, positioning cones closely together.

Form second layer over first layer, placing cones perpendicular to bottom layer, pointing in direction of underlying wire rings. Two will usually fit across together. Complete third ring layer.

As cones dry and expand, gaps will disappear. Attach tiny pinecones to fill in sparse areas.

Drill holes through nuts with fine drill bit and attach to wreath with wire.

Tuck in or clip all loose wires on back.

Make loop at back to hang wreath.

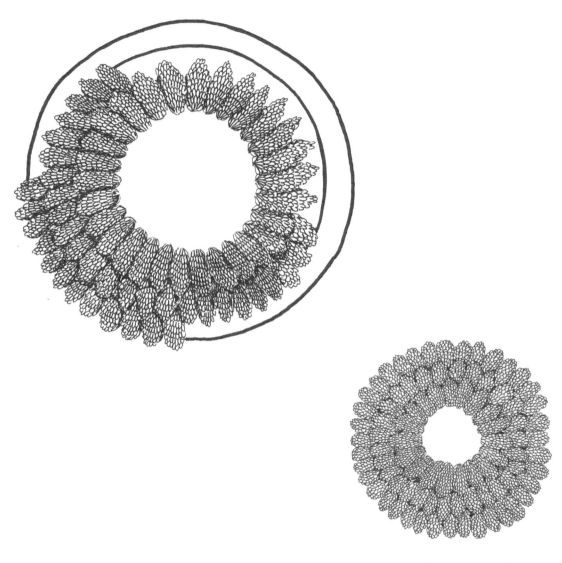

PINE CONE WREATH

Mini Wreath Candle Holder

Make this small token wreath to drop around a candle.

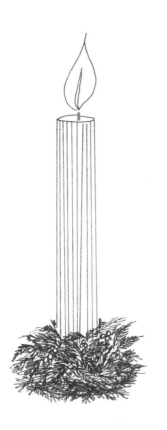

NEED

Flexible wire

Small evergreen sprigs

Floral wire

Small berry clusters, artificial or live

MAKE

Wrap wire loosely around candle base twice where wreath will rest. Snip, leaving 1" excess to fasten ends.

Using floral wire, attach evergreen sprigs by winding wire around flexible wire base. Continue around wreath, positioning shoots in same direction.

Attach berry clusters at random intervals.

Place wreath ring over candle.

Pine Cone Garland

Spread the symbol of fertility throughout your home during this bleak season.

NEED

Pinecones

Flexible wire, 2 yards

Live or artificial berry clusters

MAKE

Harvest pine cones. Bring to room temperature so they unfold like roses.

Weave wire under petals, connecting individual pine cones together.

Attach clusters of berries at random intervals.

Make loops along garland to function as hangers.

Display over mantle or mailbox.

Polish Dinner Wreath Variation

In Poland, a wreath suspended over the dining room table for a Christmas Eve feast is called the "Wilja." The heavy display contains corn, apples, feathers, and bits of colored tissue. This is a lighter alternative.

NEED

Various greenery

Feathers

Pinecones

Metal coat hanger

Ribbon, gold and red

Floral wire

Needle nose pliers

MAKE

Using pliers, bend hanger into circle shape. Connect ends

Tie three gold ribbon pieces onto wire at equal intervals.

Arrange greenery around hanger ring. Fasten with floral wire. Keep gold ribbon free to later pull toward top.

Slip feathers and pinecones through wires while working.

Feed additional gold and red ribbon through greenery.

Gather the three gold ribbon strands and fasten together.

Attach to a chandelier positioned over a table.

POLISH DINNER WREATH VARIATION

Pine Cone Crown

Wear this crown to greet holiday guests. Use it to crown a queen or king who receives the Christmas pudding coin.

NEED

4-6 large pinecones , 2-4 smaller pinecones

Flexible wire

Needle nose pliers

Clear polyurethane spray

Fake fur or felt, 4" x 24"

Plastic food wrap

MAKE

Fold felt or fake fur in half, lengthwise. Press seam. Open and lay headband right side down. Fold one side up to meet middle seam. Press. Glue underneath edges at the fold. Repeat for other side. Wrap lining around head to adjust size. Trim, leaving 1 ½" overlap. Glue right sides of ends together. Set aside.

Measure and cut wire to fit around head, leaving 4" overlap. Temporarily connect ends, loosely. Using additional wire, connect pinecones and attach to outside of circlet. Alternate large pinecones with small ones, running wire under petals.

Reel a band of plastic food wrap around the top of head to protect from sap. Adjust partially assembled crown for size. Add more pinecones where needed, alternating large and small.

Place headband on head. Wrap pinecone crown around wreath to gauge fit. Add additional pinecones if needed. Connect wire ends securely.

Lay crown on newspaper. Spray with polyurethane. Allow to dry. Leave lining and crown unconnected, or run thread around pinecones then through material.

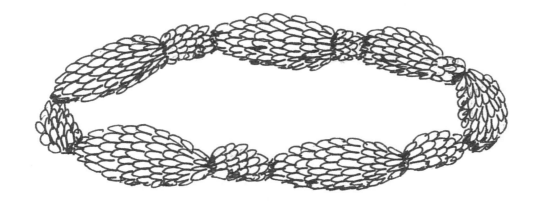

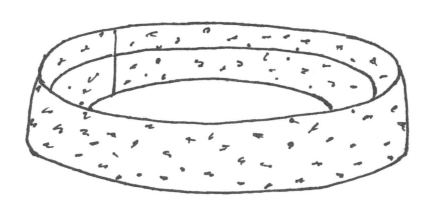

PINE CONE CROWN

Yule Log Centerpiece

This is a pretty and meaningful centerpiece, especially for those without fireplaces. Consider using four different colored candles to represent the seasons: white for winter (snow); green for spring (buds); red for summer (flowers); and gold for fall (foliage). During the week preceding the Winter Solstice, light the candles nightly. Contemplate the darkening days. Anticipate the promise of light to come.

NEED

Symmetrically shaped log, approximately 2' long

Electric drill with ¾" spade bit or butterfly drill

Hammer

Wood chisel

Ruler

Candles

MAKE

Secure log in a vise.

Using wood chisel and hammer, chip away one side of log to create level surface that can balance on table. Test result. Adjust as needed.

With log on flat surface, use ruler to mark proposed placement of candles. Return log to vise.

Drill holes where indicated, adjusting size to fit candles.

Place on table as centerpiece and insert candles.

YULE LOG CENTERPIECE

German Schnitz

Display this beautiful natural decoration over a mantle or use as a tree decoration. At season's end, hang it on a branch outside. Animals can eat the food and birds can use the string for nests.

NEED

1/2 peck apples

Raisins

Popcorn, at least one day old to facilitate stringing

Red thread, cut in several 2 yard segments

Sewing needle

MAKE

Core apples. Slice crosswise to form rings.

Feed apple rings onto string, then stretch as clothesline. Dry for several days.

Halve dried apples to resemble moon crescents.

Thread needle with thread.

String apples, raisins, and popcorn in a pleasing alternating pattern.

Make several strands.

Connect ends. Hang.

GERMAN SCHNITZ

Steaua or Star

Every day from the twenty-fourth of December to the thirty-first of December, a six cornered star was carried from house to house through Romanian villages. The custom may be related to the Roman festival known as the Atelanae or Satirae. Carry a Steaua when caroling, or display it at home as a decorative touch. Use the steaua to greet guests at the door and announce their arrival to all inside.

NEED

Several sturdy, straight green branches, approximately ¾" diameter

One long, thicker straight branch for the pole

Assorted lengths of colored ribbon

Assorted bells

Battery-powered candle

Small nail

Thin wire or twine

MAKE

Cut six 10" segments from small branches.

Construct two triangles with these segments, connecting corners with wire or twine.

Lay one triangle over another to form a star. Fasten with wire.

Attach pole to bottom of star in similar manner.

Attach battery-powered candle to pole.

Hang various lengths and colors of ribbons to corners at front of star.

Tie bells onto ribbon ends.

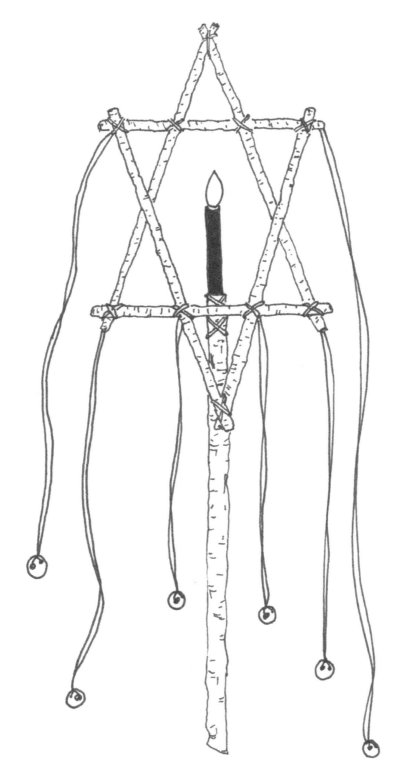

STEAUA

ANIMAL COSTUME

Animal Costume

Most people associate costumes with Halloween, but during both the Roman Saturnalia festival and Norse Sun Pageant, people dressed in costumes. English Mummers also wore costumes.

Children and adults may enjoy dressing as animals or fanciful creatures such as fairies and magicians. These outfits are easily made at home and can be worn year round. Costumes made from materials found in nature can later be returned back to the earth.

Create a costume festival for your family or friends. Prepare ancient winter recipes for dinner and enjoy eating together in costume. Invite pets into the dining area. Light lots of candles on your table.

Yardage allowance below is for an average adult basic tunic-style costume.

NEED

Fake fur, 2 yards

Thread

One big button; ribbon to use as a button loop, ¼" x 4"

MAKE

Unfold material and lay flat. Cut 6" wide strip evenly off bottom for headpiece. Set aside.

Fold large piece of material widthwise. Cut at the fold. Set aside one half.

On flat surface, fold material in half lengthwise. Cut at fold.

The four pieces of fake fur will form the costume. The large piece is the front, the two smaller pieces are the back, and the smallest piece is the headband.

With two back pieces together, fur to fur, sew a seam from bottom to 8-inches from top. Press seam open.

On flat surface, lay front of costume fur side up on a flat surface. Place costume back on top of costume front, fur to fur. Starting at one shoulder edge, pin front to back for several inches toward the center. Switch to alternate shoulder and repeat. Front side will be wider than back side.

Fold in half to determine middle of front. Mark with crosswise pin. Measure 4" to left and 4" to right of crosswise pin mark to designate costume neck area.

Sew along shoulder edge, leaving 8" opening for neck.

Try on costume. Adjust as needed. Press.

Fold over front and back neck edges. Sew and press.

With costume remaining inside out, pin sides together, leaving ample openings for arms. Try on costume. Adjust fit. Stitch and press.

Finish armhole edges in same manner as neck edge.

Center button on back neck edge and sew. Create loop with ribbon, slightly larger than button. Pin to opposite neck edge. Sew.

With right sides together, wrap headband material around head. Pin ends together. Sew. Trim. Press. Save excess to make ears.

With right sides together, fold headband in half lengthwise. Sew together open edge opposite fold, leaving 2" opening. Press seam open. Trim. Pull right side of the headband fabric through the 2" hole. Close hole using hand stitch.

To make ears, cut four identical triangle or semicircle shapes, approximately 5" diameter each.

With right sides together, sew narrow seam all around, leaving small opening. Turn ear inside out. Hand stitch opening closed. Top stitch around outside of ear to create definition. Sew onto headband.

Nature Crown

This crown has many beautiful options. Most materials can be found on a winter hike. Feathers and nuts can be purchased.

NEED

Several long green branches, or a head-sized grapevine wreath, assorted greenery, small pinecones, nuts with small holes drilled through, feathers

Floral wire, gold thread

MAKE

Soak long green branches in bathtub overnight. When pliable, bend and twist branches around each other to form a crown. Fasten with floral wire in several places. Attach greenery to crown with floral wire. Attach pinecones, nuts and feathers with gold thread.

Antler Crown

These antlers are made out of branches. Children can wear this crown to evoke the feeling of living in a winter forest. Be careful not to poke anyone's eyes.

NEED

Several long green branches, or a head-sized grapevine wreath

Floral wire

Two interesting shaped branches of equal length for antlers

Clear polyurethane spray

MAKE

Soak long green branches in bathtub overnight.

When pliable, bend and twist branches around each other to form a crown. Fasten with floral wire in several places.

Using floral wire, fasten antler branches to sides of crown.

Spray wreath and antlers with polyurethane spray.

Allow to dry.

ANTLER CROWN

GERMAN LICHSTOCK

German Lichstock, Light Stick, or Pyramid

The German wooden Yule pyramid called lichstock or light stick, originally featured shelves containing candles, gifts, figurines, pastries, and ornaments. In seventeenth century Germany, a decorated light stick was positioned on the floor next to a bare evergreen. Lichstocks were sometimes given as gifts. The British adopted this tradition, adding apples, nuts and gilded evergreen boughs to their light sticks. In the 1800s, a wooden pyramid was often used in place of a Christmas tree.

NEED

Several long and sturdy uniformly sized branches; assorted pinecones

Tiny battery-powered candles or a string of electric lights

Gold spray paint (optional); Red, green, and white satin ribbon, 1" x 6'

Electric drill with small drill bits; flexible wire

MAKE

Assess length of collected branches. Cut four 18" pieces. Place end of one branch in a vise. Drill a small hole through branch ½" from end. Repeat with two remaining branches. Feed wire through branch holes, winding firmly but flexibly around all three branches.

Determine desired pyramid leg spread, then measure distance between each leg at level where two horizontal supports will be positioned. Mark these locations on both vertical branches and horizontal supports. Drill holes where indicated.

Connect all branches with wire. Once pyramid is erected, weave evergreen boughs in and out of structure. Attach pinecones to evergreens with wire, thread, or twine. Place one pinecone on pyramid top. Tie ribbon streamers onto each leg.

Drape electric lights over greens. If using battery-powered candles, balance them on branches, using boughs for support.

Celtic

Celtic Cross Ornament or Pendant

The sun symbol or Celtic Cross is believed to have originated about 3000 BCE in the western Carpathian region, far from the British Isles. Appearing first on pottery, it was later seen on metal work during the Beaker Culture. Because it was common on gold objects, experts believe it was a symbol for the sun. It spread across Europe and into the British Isles. Irish people used it so frequently that it became a trademark of their work.

NEED

Self-hardening modeling clay or bakeable molding compound

Clear polyurethane spray

Black silk cord, 6" for ornament and 24" for pendant

MAKE

Roll two thin 9" clay snakes. Form into two smooth circles. One will be top and one will be bottom.

Roll two thicker 3" clay snakes.

Lay one circle on flat surface. Place a 3" snake over the center of the circle.

Place second 3" snake over first, forming a cross. Trim overhanging edges.

Position remaining circle over cross. Moisten hands, then gently pat outside and inside of ornament, sealing top and bottom circles together.

Use a pencil tip to make a hole in top of circle, slightly larger than necessary to accommodate silk cord. Allow to dry for several days, or bake according to instructions.

Spray with polyurethane spray. Allow to dry. Thread cord through hole. Hang.

CELTIC CROSS ORNAMENT

Orange Peel Spectacles

The intent of the "Lord of Misrule" in merry old England was to make a mockery of the Church in as many ways possible. The "lord" entered with partners in crime, disrupting the ongoing service, reading prayer books upside down, and performing assorted antics. Orange peel spectacles were a popular prop. Display these conversation starters as favors on dinner plates.

NEED

One navel orange per spectacles

Foral wire

MAKE

Using basic kitchen knife, cut through peel, but not into orange. Form a spiral by starting at the navel, carefully creating a continuously connected circle to reach the opposite end. Keep uniform the width of space between each circling row.

Gently peel skin away from pulp.

Secure the shape with floral wire.

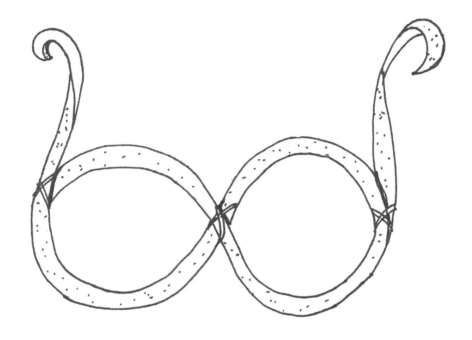

ORANGE PEEL SPECTACLES

Kissing Wreath

This popular decoration garnered attention during the twelve days of Christmas. A Victorian era ceiling easily accommodated a wreath, but the garland can also be hung over the frame of any frequently used door, allowing guests to be kissed as they walk underneath. Gifts attached to the wreath or bough can be distributed and replaced, once removed.

Wreath

NEED

One small evergreen wreath

Mistletoe

Red ribbon, ½" x 18'

Embellishments such as assorted small ornaments, mistletoe, tiny wrapped gifts including candies, money, or lightweight tokens

MAKE

Cut ribbon into pieces; four 4', one 2'.

Gather ends of four 4' pieces and tie together into knot. Lay on flat surface. Spread four pieces into four different directions.

Center wreath over four splayed ribbons. Loosely wind each ribbon once around wreath, keeping four points equally distant from one another.

Gather and pull up four ribbon ends. Tie into knot.

Hang wreath from high ceiling, tall hallway or doorway, or hanging plant hook.

Loop 2' ribbon at wreath center where longer ribbons intersect. Pull ends of two foot ribbon together. Attach cluster of mistletoe. Tie ribbon into bow.

Using gold thread, hang various presents, ornaments, and mistletoe from wreath.

Kissing Garland

NEED

Sturdy stick; 3' long, evergreen boughs; embellishments such as assorted small ornaments, mistletoe, tiny wrapped gifts including candies, money, or lightweight tokens

Floral wire; gold thread; red ribbon, ½" x 6'

MAKE

Trim stick to fit over doorway frame. Using florist wire, attach various greenery to branch. Add loops at intervals for hanging above doorway.

Weave ribbon through boughs. Using gold thread, hang ornaments, presents, and mistletoe from garland. Drive 2-3 nails inconspicuously into doorway frame. Hang.

Mini Yule Log Place Favors

Make these take-home reminders of a warm holiday gathering.

NEED

Several uniform branches, approximately ¾" diameter

Gold wire

Red ribbon segments, ¼" x 12" per favor

Tiny berries or artificial flowers

MAKE

Saw branches into 6" segments.

Attach berries or flowers by artfully winding wire and ribbon around each log.

Place at table settings.

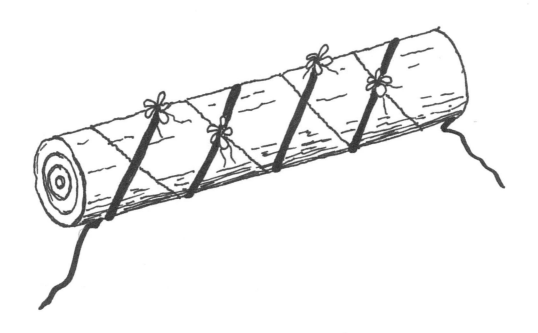

Jingle Bell Ankle and Wrist Bands for Mummers and Others

Noise was believed to frighten evil spirits lurking in the frigid dark.

NEED

Felt strip, 4" x 12" for adult ankle

Felt strip, 4" x 10" for adult wrist

Jingle bells

Ribbon, four strips, 1" x 8"

Contrasting color thread

MAKE

Adjust size. Trim ankle and wrist felt strips to fit adult or child. Band ends should be short of meeting so ribbon can connect them.

Fold felt in half lengthwise. Sew halves together along open edge.

To make ties, sew ribbon strip securely to middle of each strip end.

Sew jingle bells onto felt.

Fasten to wrists and ankles.

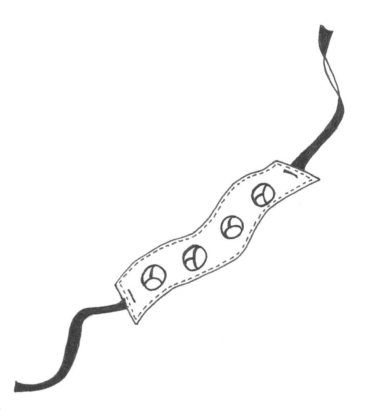

Mantle Poem

Fasten twigs together to make a rustic frame for this Robert Herrick poem about the Yule log.

NEED

Twigs for frame, two 6" and two 8"

Rigid poster board rectangle, 6" x 8"

Black Marker

Gold thread, four 36" pieces

Sewing needle

Awl

MAKE

With pencil, measure 1" from poster board edge, then draw border. Carefully puncture two small holes outside margins of each corner of poster board.

Within margin, find midpoint, then draw horizontal line for text guideline. Draw four lines above midpoint and five lines below. Using pencil, skip first line of poster board, then begin writing the following poem, indenting every other line:

Kindle the Christmas brand and then

Till sunset let it burn,

which, quenched, then lay it up again,

Till Christmas next return.

Part must be kept werewith to tend

The Christmas log next year;

And where it is safely kept, the fiend

Can do no mischief here.

Outline pencil margin with marker. Trace over poem with marker.

Cut twigs; two 8" and two 6".

Fold 36" gold thread in half, creating double thickness. Thread one end of 18" gold thread through margin hole on one corner of poster board. Thread other end of thread through second margin hole. Pull threads through front of poster board until ends meet. Repeat process in remaining three corners.

Place 6" twig vertically along poster board, then attach with gold thread. Repeat on other side. Place 8" twig horizontally along poster board, over vertical twig, then attach with gold thread. Tie gold thread securely. Trim. Place poem on fireplace mantle.

Kindle the Christmas brand and then
    Till sunset let it burn,
which, quenched, then lay it up again,
    Till Christmas next return.

Part must be kept werewith to tend
    The Christmas log next year;
And where it is safely kept, the fiend
    Can do no mischief here.
                    Robert Herrick

Mummer's Mask

Mummers and others can wear this mask. Alternatively, create a decorative conversation piece by attaching three ribbons to the headband, then suspending it from ceiling.

NEED

Assorted fabrics, old sheets, clean rags, old ties, and ribbons, cut or torn into strips, 2" x 18-36"

Fabric for headband, 6" x 24"

Jingle bells

Thread

Sewing machine

MAKE

With headband strip right side down, turn lengthwise edges under ½". Press. Fold headband strip in half, lengthwise, right sides together. Press. Open and lay flat, right side down.

Leaving 4" free on each end, arrange and pin streamers of varying lengths to turned-up edge of headband. Streamers should face right side up. Headband remains wrong side up.

Sew streamers onto headband.

Adjust headband fit on head. Attach and sew additional streamers if needed, leaving 1" margin on both ends for seam.

With right sides together, sew end seams.

Fold one lengthwise headband edge over the other, wrong sides and turned-up edges matching. Pin. Sew closely along outside turned up edge seam.

Tie bells onto ribbon ends, or thread and attach randomly to ends of streamers.

Jiffy Mummer's Mask

Measure, cut, and decorate heavy cardboard for headband.

Glue or staple multicolored crepe paper streamers all around headband.

Connect headband ends.

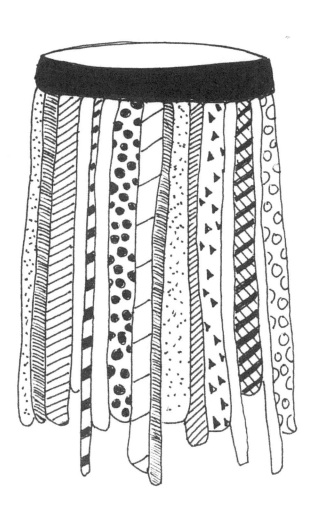

Mistletoe Mobile

As a sign of peace and friendship, Mistletoe is a fitting addition to any holiday home. According to Roman mythology, it contains the seed of fire. A branch of it became known as the "golden bough" when Aeneas held it to light his way through the underworld of Hades. Other purported mistletoe attributes: antidote against poison; fertility enhancer; protection against premature birth; cure for epilepsy; ulcers and many other ills.

The people of Northern Europe believed that if two enemies stood underneath mistletoe together, they would become friends.

(Mistletoe is not safe to eat. Care should be taken around children and pets.)

NEED

One slender green branch, 3' long; several bunches of mistletoe

Floral wire

Red ribbon, ½" x 12'

Gold thread

MAKE

Cut side shoots off branch. Soak overnight in bathtub.

Bend branch into desired circle size. Secure with floral wire.

Cut ribbon into six 24" pieces. Fold one ribbon in half, then drape over branch, feeding ends through the loop to secure to mobile. Repeat with other ribbons, spacing evenly around the branch circle. Tie bows at end of each ribbon. Use gold thread to tie mistletoe to each bow.

Cut three pieces of gold thread, 48" each. Fold each piece in half. There will be three 24" pieces. At equal distances apart, tie gold thread to branch circle to hang mobile level. Tie together at top.

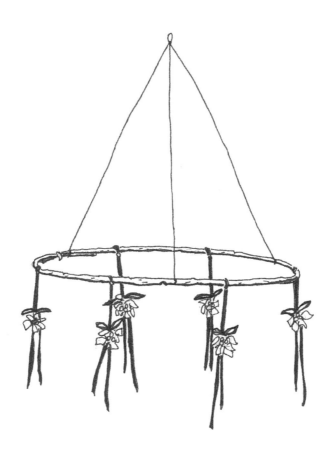

MISTLETOE MOBILE

Additional Creative Ideas

Greeting Cards

Select an ancient custom or little known fact about the winter season to use as a theme for your card. Find or create a related illustration about the custom and print a caption beneath it.

NEED

Card stock paper and envelope

Permanent markers, black and colored

MAKE

Fold and trim paper to fit into envelope

Design cover illustration in pencil

Outline and color illustration with markers

Add caption

For example: POLAZNIK

Caption below cover illustration: On Christmas morning in Yugoslavia, the Polaznik (first person to arrive) threw a handful of wheat at everyone as a charm to ensure health, wealth, and fertile crops in the coming year.

Caption inside card: May your year be fruitful!

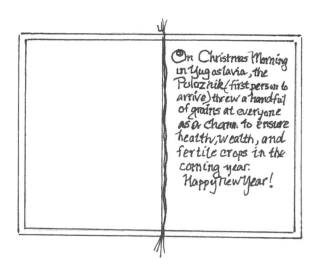

GREETING CARDS

Holly

Holly represents the old year and should be removed from the home after New Year's Day to avoid bad luck. Holly also symbolizes domestic happiness, foresight, friendship and good wishes.

Holly Hairclips

NEED

A metal hair clip from a craft store

Floral wire

Holly sprig

MAKE

Attach holly piece to hairclip with floral wire.

Apple Candle Place Settings

An apple represents harvest bounty. The candle represents the light of the new year.

NEED

Red and green symmetrical apples, one per place setting

Standard dinner candle for each apple

Apple corer

MAKE

Core apple, carving hole large enough to hold candle.

Trim bottom of apple to level.

Place candle in hole. Adjust fit by wrapping foil around candle base, then inserting candle into apple.

Arrange apple candles at each place setting. At breakfast, lunch, or supper, ask each person to make a wish for the new year, then light his or her respective candle.

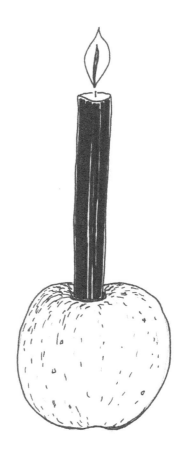

Greenery

To ancient people, a grove of trees was a sacred place and site of many rituals and ceremonies. Plant a circle of evergreen trees to establish a sacred grove for generations to follow.

A solstice tree embodies the elements of earth, water, air, and fire. It grows from a seed in earth, drinks water, reaches skyward, and becomes a torch if struck by lightning.

Decorate your tree on Winter Solstice Eve with ornaments representative of ancient celebrations and pagan roots. Spend time around the tree before placing gifts under it. Make some gifts intangibles—like certificates for good deeds. Offer a basketful of gifts for everyone: games to be played together; food to enjoy as a group; passes to a holiday festival; or special items to physically pamper. Hold hands with others and focus on the gift of companionship.

After Christmas, move the tree outside into a pot of dirt, or prop rocks around the trunk so it will stand erect. Decorate it again, this time for the benefit of birds. Add popcorn garlands and hang suet and peanut butter balls from outer branches.

Allow the tree to decay or burn in a summer solstice bonfire. Save one branch to use in the next year's yule fire.

In Norway, families join hands and sing, circling the Christmas tree. After the holidays, the tree is fashioned into a bird pole by removing all branches except a few at the top. It is placed in a large area cleared of snow, where sheaves of grain are arranged around its base.

In parts of Germany and Austria, only the tip of the evergreen was hung upside down from the rafters to decorate the home. The tip was decorated with apples, gilded nuts, and pieces of red paper.

Before electricity, candles were used to light trees. In the 1700s, a twelve foot tree could be covered with over 400 candles. Servants hovered nearby with wet mops and buckets of water.

Greenery Hints

Fresh greenery is a way to connect with nature during winter months. To keep greens fresh up to two weeks, make long vertical cuts in stems, then soak overnight in cool water. Moisture can be sealed into holly and ivy by dipping sprig ends into candle wax, or entire branches into clear floor wax. Allow both to dry on newspaper.

Ornaments

Many ornaments, whether handmade or received as gifts, become more special as time passes. A descriptive note stored with the ornament records its history and makes for good reading in future years.

Acorn Basket Ornament

Oak forests once covered Great Britain. Acorns were so plentiful that acorn meal was used to make bread. Fill these dough ornaments with nuts.

NEED

2 cups flour

1 cup salt

1 egg

Oven proof custard cups (one per ornament), or aluminum foil shaped into molds

Vegetable oil

Acorns

Polyurethane spray

Ribbon, ¼" x 12" pieces, 3 pieces per ornament

MAKE

Preheat oven to 300 degrees.

Grease outside of custard cups or shaped foil .In large bowl, combine 2 cups flour and 1 cup salt. Gradually add 1 cup water and stir well. On lightly floured surface, knead dough 5 minutes, or until no longer sticky. Divide dough. Roll out 8 thin snakes per basket. Basket weave dough around cups or foil molds. Trim long ends. Place baskets onto foil or parchment covered cookie tray. Brush dough with egg yolk.

Bake in 300 degree oven for 1 hour until quite firm. Remove tray from oven. Allow ornaments to cool completely. Remove cups or foil. Spray dough baskets with polyurethane spray. Allow to dry. Thread ribbon through ornament edges at three places, adjusting to balance basket. Gather ends and tie together into bow. Fill with acorns.

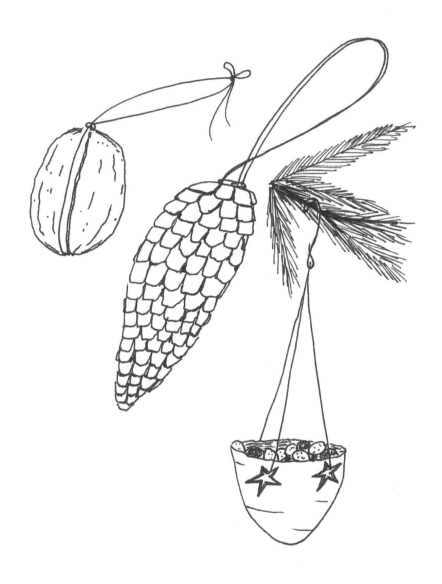

NATURE SCAVENGER ORNAMENTS

Nut Ornaments

Raw nuts hung from a tree as ornaments evoke the simplicity of nature and its hidden treasures. If you live in a city and can't search for whole nuts in the woods, buy them at the grocery around Thanksgiving when they are usually available.

NEED

Acorns, walnuts, Brazil nuts

Super glue

Thread or thin ribbon, red and gold

MAKE

Measure and cut ribbon or thread to fit around nut allowing excess length for suspension.

Glue area around nut where thread will be attached.

Press ribbon/thread onto glue and nut.

Let dry.

Tie ribbon/thread snuggly at top of nut. Create hanging loop by tying ends into bow.

Nature Scavenger Ornament

A simple, but stunning ornament is one pinecone hung from a thin red ribbon. It looks beautiful year after year. During late summer and fall, search for interesting pine cones or seed pods to use as ornaments. Fasten ribbon onto one end by weaving under and over protrusions, or glue on ribbon instead.

HAND PAINTED ORNAMENTS

Hand Painted Ornaments

Hand painting ornaments makes a great excuse to gather friends and family.

NEED

Heavy gauge watercolor paper

Stiff cardboard

Felt

Drinking glass, for tracing

Pencil

Markers, water colors, or acrylic paints

Glue

Ribbon, ¼" x 12"

MAKE

Use drinking glass and pencil to trace circles on watercolor paper, stiff cardboard, and felt. Cut circles from cardboard and felt. Leave watercolor paper intact.

Draw or paint designs or scenes inside circles on watercolor paper.

When dry, cut circles from watercolor paper.

Glue cardboard circles to watercolor circle backs. Trim as needed.

Glue felt circles to cardboard circle backs.

Measure and cut ribbon to wrap around outside of circles, leaving sufficient length to suspend ornament by loop and make bow.

Apply glue around outside ornament edge. Allow to dry.

Tie knot at top of ornament, then fashion a bow at end of ribbon loop.

Hang from tree or chandelier.

FRUIT ORNAMENTS

Fruit Ornament

This ornament may be too heavy for a tree but it can be hung from the ceiling or displayed with others in a bowl.

NEED

Whole cloves

Small apples and small oranges

Ribbon, ¼" x 18"

MAKE

Push cloves into skins of apple or orange in an interesting pattern.

Using two ribbon pieces, wrap around opposite sides, then tie at top. Tie again for loop. Hang.

Alternatively, arrange decorated fruit as a fragrant display in glass bowl, on mantle, or table.

Stained Glass Ornaments

To prevent ornament edges from curling, store between book pages or thick cardboard.

NEED

Black construction paper

Clear adhesive shelf lining paper

Colored tissue paper, cut into 1/2" squares

Gold colored thread

Pencil

Box cutter

Scissors

MAKE

Measure 6" long shape for ornament frame on construction paper. With pencil, draw line ½" inside and around ornament edge. Draw design inside frame area, without severing connection between design and frame. Cut around outside ornament edge, freeing ornament from paper. Cut design within frame area using a box cutter.

Place ornament frame with cut-out design on empty construction paper. Trace around design with pencil. This will be the ornament back. Cut around edge of back ornament and cut inside for design.

Cut one piece of shelf lining paper twice as large as ornament frame and lay on flat surface. Remove backing from shelf liner, exposing sticky side.

Place top frame on the far left side of shelf paper. Fill frame with ½" color tissue paper pieces, allowing them to stick to the adhesive shelf lining. Create a simple geometric design or an elaborate winter scene. All tissue paper should touch the shelf liner.

Make a loop of gold thread to hang the ornament. Use a dot of glue to hold it in place. Allow to dry.

Put frame back over design to cover bottom frame, matching edges. Next, fold right side of shelf liner over left edge of frame, covering entire ornament. Leave a small margin around outside of frame so shelf liner can adhere to itself. Trim edges. Hang.

Holly Ornament

The best holly ornament is a fresh sprig with ribbon tied around. This is something more permanent.

NEED

Green felt, 8"x8" square per ornament

Small red wooden beads, 1/2" diameter, three beads per ornament

Needle

Red thread

Green ribbon, ¼" x 10" per ornament

MAKE

Using stencil, cut out several leaves of green felt; three per ornament.

Spread three leaves on flat surface, slightly overlapping bases.

With needle and red thread, sew one small red wooden bead through base of leaves, catching all three together. Continue this process with two remaining beads.

Sew a loop of green ribbon through base of leaves and hang.

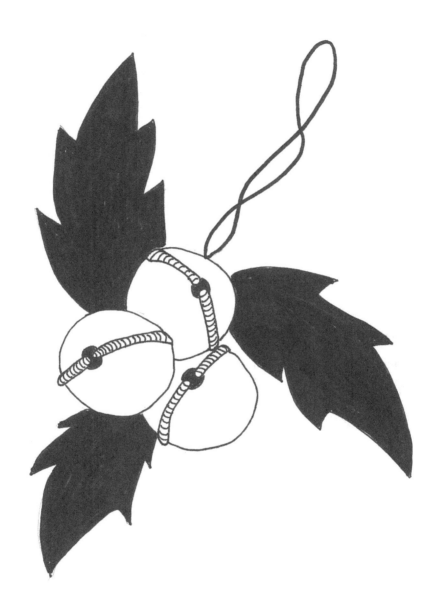

HOLLY ORNAMENT

Solstice Tree

It's nice to display seasonal pottery but not loaded with candies and cookies. There are healthier ways to create a festive atmosphere.

NEED

Ceramic bowl or jar

Sand or dirt to fill

Tree branch, sturdy and dry

Tiny ornaments, purchased or handmade (tiny dough birds, stars, suns and moons, cranberries)

Candy pieces

Gold thread

Needle

MAKE

Fill bowl with sand or dirt. Position branch.

Hang ornaments onto tree. Fasten dough birds with wire. Hang stars, suns, moons, and cranberry ornaments from branches by passing thread through each with sewing needle.

Hang candy pieces from tree. Select a piece on each day leading to the solstice.

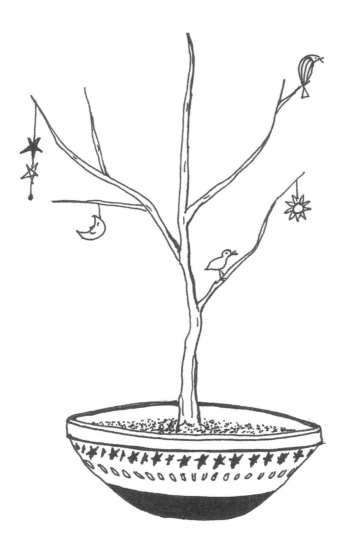

SOLSTICE TREE

Scented Tea Cushion

When windows are closed for months at a time, air can grow stale. These aromatic cushions can be used at home, or given away as gifts.

NEED

Printed fabric, 6"x6" for individual cups, and 9"x9" for teapots

Lace or cord for edging, 24" or 36"

Polyester batting, 6"x6" or 9"x9"

Potpourri—buy or make from dried herbs from your garden

Needle and thread and/or sewing machine

MAKE

Lay one square right side up on flat surface. Arrange lace or cord along edges so that outside edges of lace or cord face toward middle of square. Lay second square on top of first square with lace, right sides together.

Pin. All lace or cord should be even with material edges.

Pin square of batting on top of prepared squares.

Sew around edges, leaving 1 1/2" opening on one edge.

Turn cushion right side out.

Run potpourri briefly through blender or mini-chopper, or wrap inside small, double layered paper bag and pound on counter.

Using 4-6 tablespoons per cushion, fill cushion with potpourri, shaking back and forth to distribute through the square.

Hand sew remaining open edge.

A warm mug or pot will activate the scent.

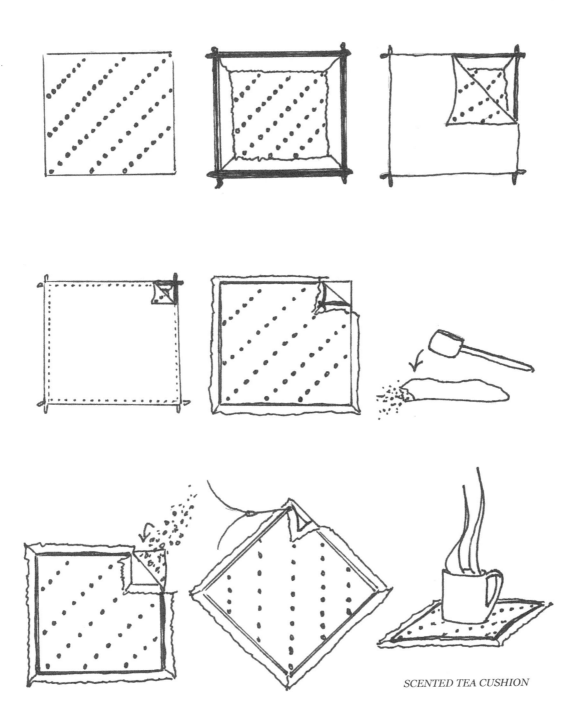

SCENTED TEA CUSHION

Solstice Scent

NEED

2 cups water

8 whole cloves

2 cinnamon sticks

Peel from one orange and one lemon, cut into pieces.

A small, heavy pot

MAKE

Combine water and other ingredients in pot. Simmer uncovered. Add more water as needed.

Citrus Bath

In Japan, people enjoy citrus baths around the time of the winter solstice.

NEED

6 each, lemons, limes, oranges

MAKE

Slice thinly each of 5 lemons, limes and oranges.

Slice remaining fruit into halves.

Close bathtub drain. Place fruit into bottom of tub. Fill bath water with comfortably hot water. When bath is full, squeeze juice from fruit halves into water. Twist peels over water to release zest.

Winter Solstice Mobile

Plan ahead. Collect items in fall so mobile can be assembled later.

NEED

12 pieces from nature—nuts, small sprigs, leaves, feathers

One sturdy green twig, 48" long

Red ribbon, 1/4" x 72"; gold thread; florist wire, clear adhesive shelf lining paper

Power drill and small drill bit; vise

MAKE

Soak branch in bathtub water overnight.

Place nuts in vise to drill thread holes. Drill through.

Cut shelf liner piece twice as big as leaf. Tear off protective paper. Place leaf on one side and wrap liner over top. Trim edges.

Bend branch into a circle, 12" diameter or smaller. Overlap ends to make sturdy. Secure with florist wire.

Cut 72" red ribbon into three 24" pieces. Fold each piece in half.

Wrap looped end of one ribbon around branch ring. Bring two ends through loop so that ribbon holds branch securely. Repeat with remaining ribbons, spacing evenly around ring. Pull ribbon ends up and tie together. Hang to test balance of the mobile. Ring should hang parallel to the ground. Leave hanging.

Cut 12 pieces of gold thread, each 12" long. Attach to ring at even intervals.

Tie pieces of nature to strings, maintaining mobile symmetry. A nut on one side will require two others at opposite points to balance. Vary string lengths to create interest and achieve balance. Consider how the balance of nature can be easily disrupted.

WINTER SOLSTICE MOBILE

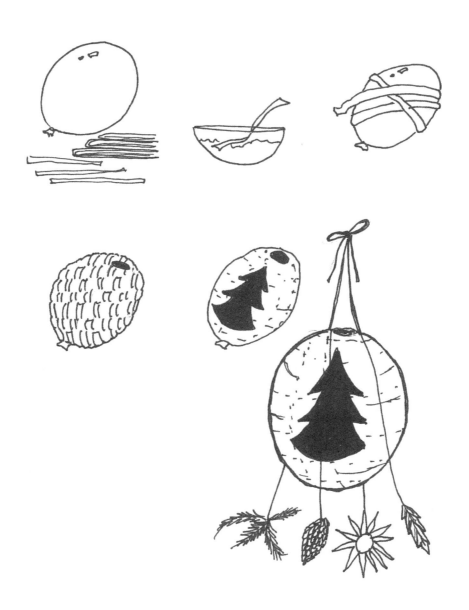

PIÑATA

Piñata

A piñata is part of winter festivities in Mexico, Central and South America.

This is a papier-mache project.

NEED

One large balloon, 11" or larger

Several newspapers

1 cup flour

2 cups water

Pinecones and small sprigs of evergreens

Paint, deep blue and tree green colors

Paint brush

Construction paper, one yellow sheet and one green sheet

Red satin ribbon, ¼" x 96" and ½" x 48"

Small seasonal-themed stickers

Assorted bite-size candy to fill piñata

A sturdy swatting stick

MAKE

Inflate balloon.

Tear newspaper into long strips, 2 inches wide.

Prepare papier-mache paste by combining 1 cup flour with 2 cups water.

Dip newspaper strips into papier-mache mix. Run fingers over strip to remove excess. Apply strips to outside of balloon, gradually creating four layer thickness. Allow to dry several days.

When dry, cut a hole in the top of the piñata to add candy later. (The balloon will have likely popped or shriveled.)

Paint piñata exterior blue. Allow to dry. Paint a large green evergreen, or several smaller trees, over the blue. Apply second coat if needed.

Cut several 4" tall green trees and yellow suns from construction paper. Punch a hole in the top of each. Cut 1/4" ribbon into eight 12" inch pieces. Tie a pinecone and /or evergreen sprig to four ribbons. Attach construction paper trees and suns to remaining ribbons.

On top of the piñata, puncture two holes at opposite sides approximately 1" from the hole into which candy will be deposited.

Thread the 1/2" ribbon through the two holes. Match ends of ribbon and tie together.

Attach pinecones, evergreens, trees and suns to ½" ribbon.

Fill piñata with candy.

Hang piñata from a beam. Let blindfolded guest swat at it using the sturdy stick.

Candles

Candles are ancient sun symbols. During the Roman Kalends festival's sigillariorum celebratis fair, a candle gift was given as a charm to encourage the sun's post-solstice power. Romans also celebrated a holiday called Cerealia to honor Ceres, the goddess who searched by candlelight for her daughter Prosperpina. A candle-carrying procession made its way through the street to commemorate this odyssey. Also honored with a candle display was the goddess Februa, mother of Mars. Ultimately, the Church managed to transfer focus of these established candle festivals from the sun to Mary. Candlemas, the February 2nd procession and blessing of candles, is a relic of these faithful pagan roots.

Lighting candles, versus using electric light late in the afternoon, is an instructive adventure. Providing more than ambience, they remind us that light in this simple form was not only practical, but helped us feel less lonely in the cold dark afternoons and evenings. Gathering in the glow can remind us how much we need comfort from each other amidst the winter chill.

As the candles burn and become smaller, consider and appreciate the fact that our ancestors made their own candles—first securing the necessary raw material, and then methodically producing them on a regular basis.

When candle making was a standard household chore, the basic materials used were beeswax and tallow. Beeswax comes from the honeycomb of bees, a substance with a wide array of visual beauty and aroma. The honeycomb was melted in hot water, then strained and cooled. Tallow is fat harvested from sheep or cows but can also be derived from the fruit of the bay tree. An element in tallow called stearin hardens wax and helps a candle burn longer. Today, paraffin wax is more commonly used than beeswax, but stearin is still added.

A Solstice or Yule season would not be complete without the warm glow of candlelight. Lean how to make and decorate candles and become immersed in the spirit of the return of the sun.

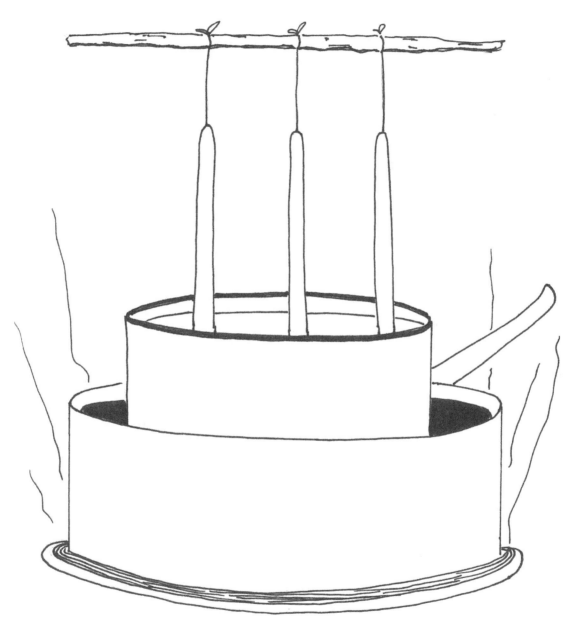

TAPER CANDLES

Taper Candles

NEED

Sufficient beeswax to make the number of candles desired

A large pot of water

A tall can (such as a coffee can) to fit into the pot of water

Wick string

Pencil or straight stick, 12" or longer

MAKE

Cut wick string to a length double the desired candle height.

Tie one end of wick string to pencil or stick. Attach no more than three strings per stick, spaced 2" apart.

Next to stove, set up area for candles to hang while they harden. This can be done by placing two chairs together with newspaper underneath, or two piles of books, or any other configuration to accommodate the span of the stick with candles hanging from it.

Place wax into can. Place can into pot of water.

Heat water gently until wax melts. Keep over very low flame to maintain liquefaction.

Hold each end of stick or pencil, then dip wick string into melted beeswax. Remove in a smooth motion, then hang immediately from improvised set up of books or chairs. Alternatively, dip candles into a bucket of cool water to speed set-up time, then hang.

Allow to cool.

Repeat dipping process until candles achieve desired thickness.

These candles will burn quickly but will smell delightful.

Molded Candles

To make uniquely shaped candles, use tiny plastic containers, clean egg shells, or any container that will safely hold hot wax. Sand is a beautiful and stable mold. To make an appealing candle shape, simply press the design you would like into sand and flatten bottom area so candle base will be level. Follow instructions below for wicks, then fill the sand cavity with hot wax. When wax has cooled completely, remove candle and trim wick string.

NEED

Candle wax, old crayons, or similarly colored candle bits

Candle molds, bought or found

Wick string

Small metal washers

Pencils or sticks, twice the width of candle mold surface

Pot full of water

Can that fits into pot, large enough to melt quantity of wax

Popsicle stick or other clean poker

MAKE

Cut piece of wick string 12" long. Attach one end loosely to pencil or suspension stick. Tie a washer onto the other end of the wick string. Set aside.

Position molds over wax-paper-covered level surface. Holding suspension stick, drop washer ends of wick into empty molds. Adjust length of wick on stick so pencil or stick rests securely on outside edges of mold.

Put wax into can. Put can into pot of water.

Heat water gently until wax melts. Keep on very low flame to maintain liquefied state.

Carefully pour small amount of wax into each mold, pouring more to side of mold to avoid bubbles. Candle will be built gradually by adding additional wax increments. Wax will settle as it cools. Use clean stick to poke small hole around wick, then pour a little more wax into that hole. Continue doing this every hour until no more wax is needed.

Leave candle in mold for one week

Release candle from mold. If difficult, refrigerate candle for several hours so wax will contract from mold. To burn longer and chip less, place candle in freezer for a few hours prior to use.

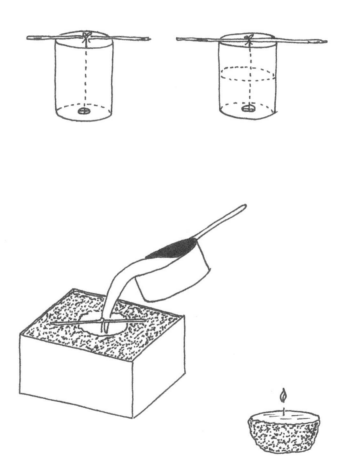

Yule Candle

In England, the Yule log was often replaced by a large candle, big enough to burn for the entire day. The candle was lit at night and signaled the start of drinking and merrymaking. When the candle burned out, the party would end and the long winter's nap would begin. Whether hand-made or purchased, a striking design can be affixed to the outside of the Yule candle.

NEED

Sheets of beeswax, dark green, deep blue, and yellow

Heavy paper for pattern template

Knife and cutting surface

MAKE

Beeswax is naturally soft and easily molded by the warmth of hands or hairdryer. Draw two evergreen trees and a sun circle on heavy paper, proportionate to candle size. Cut paper shapes to serve as patterns for beeswax designs. Place paper patterns over beeswax. Using sharp knife on cutting surface, cut green tree and yellow sun shapes out of wax.

Warm blue sheet with hands until pliable. Wrap sheet around outside of candle. Because it is background for the tree and sun, it does not need to completely cover candle. Seal edges by running fingers along seam until indiscernible.

Warm yellow wax sun circle in hands. When soft, place on the upper middle section of blue backdrop. Cut several thin yellow wax strips and place rays around sun.

Warm green tree shapes. Press onto lower left section of blue backdrop.

Light candle. When extinguished, allow outside to cool to preventing design smearing.

YULE CANDLE

Seed Candles

Give thanks for past harvests and hope for the new year's crops with these candles.

NEED

Large white pillar candle

Sheet of colored beeswax

Hairdryer

Sheet of foil

Variety of seeds and nuts such as pumpkin, sesame, millet, mung beans, brown and red lentils, adzuki, black beans, corn kernels, unpopped popcorn, white rice, brown rice, and wild rice

MAKE

Arrange and sort seeds and nuts. On paper, make rough sketch of seed design.

Measure pillar candle circumference and height.

Cut beeswax piece to specifications.

Place beeswax on foil. Hold hairdryer set on low 12" from wax. Wave over until wax softens. Once pliable, pick up wax and wrap around candle, sealing edges. Allow to cool.

With blow dryer at low setting and at 12" distance, slightly warm small section of newly applied wax. Press seeds or nuts onto wax, following design plan. Material will fall out if wax is too warm. Repeat until complete.

Always allow candle to cool completely before touching.

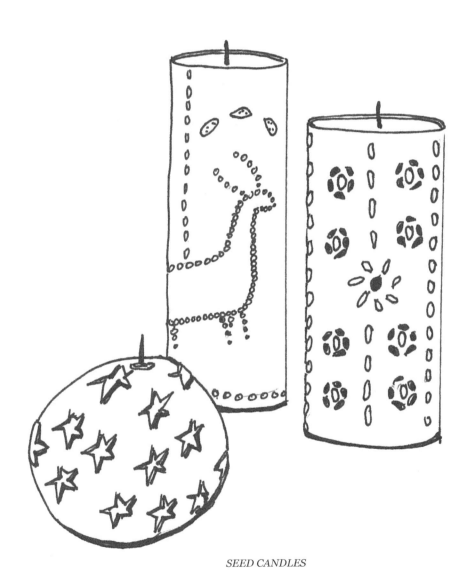

SEED CANDLES

Glitter Candles

These candles can be simple or elaborate, as time allows.

NEED

Nonflammable glue

Colored glitter

Pillar or taper-style candles

Disposable or old candle holder

Wax paper

MAKE

Cover work surface with double sheet of wax paper.

Place candle in candle holder.

Apply glue sparingly to candle in desired pattern. If using additional glitter colors, apply first color pattern only.

Shake glitter over top of candle so it sticks to glue. Or sprinkle glue onto candle while tilting and turning.

Recover excess glitter by removing top sheet of wax paper, then funnel glitter into original container.

Repeat process with additional glitter colors.

GLITTER CANDLES

Wood Candle Holder

This simple reminder of nature grows lovelier every year. Search for a branch in autumn woods before snow covers the ground.

NEED

Tree branch, approximately 3" in diameter

Saw

Sandpaper

Power drill with 3/4" spade bit, or butterfly drill

Vise-grip

Wood oil

Felt

Glue

MAKE

Wash, clean, and dry branch.

Cut desired number of 1" thick pieces from branch.

Sand tops and bottoms of pieces.

Place one piece in a vise. Using ¾" bit, drill hole through center. Test candle fit and adjust as needed.

Sand opening smooth. Wipe away sawdust.

Rub sanded surfaces sparingly with wood oil. Allow to dry.

Place wood candle holder onto piece of felt. Trace around outside circumference. Cut felt circle. Glue to bottom of holder.

WOOD CANDLE HOLDER

Clay Candle Holder

Personalize each holder.

NEED

Self-hardening clay

Toothpicks

Paint and paint brushes (optional)

Clear polyurethane spray

Felt

Candles

MAKE

Form clay into block or oval shape, 2" thick.

Push base of candle almost completely through clay base. The clay surrounding candle should be at least ½" for stability.

Use toothpick to make decorative designs such as acorns, trees, or suns on clay base.

Allow base to dry several days.

Once dry, paint if desired, or spray with polyurethane and allow to dry again.

Trace outline of base onto felt. Cut piece. Glue onto bottom.

Insert candle into base.

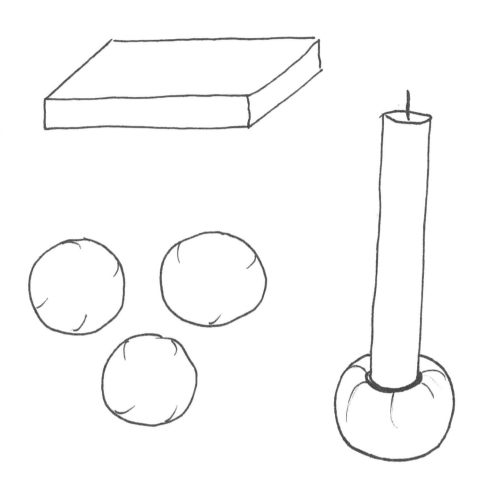

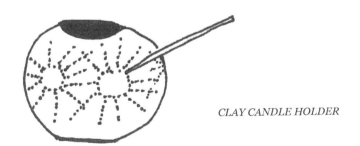

CLAY CANDLE HOLDER

Candle Wreaths

These can be used year after year.

NEED

Green felt, 8"x8" piece per wreath

Small red wooden beads

Elastic, 1/8" wide

Yarn sewing needle

Scissors

MAKE

Cut felt leaf shapes proportionate to candle size.

Cut lengths of elastic 2" longer than circumference of candle base.

Thread elastic through yarn needle. Alternately thread leaves and beads onto elastic, achieving desired effect.

Loosely tie elastic ends and adjust wreath to candle. Secure ends. Trim elastic.

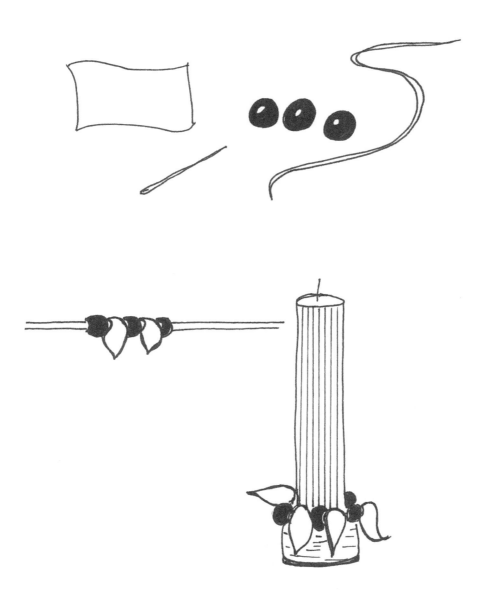

CANDLE WREATH

SOLAR CANDLE DISPLAY

Solar Candle Display

The discs in this display represent the sun and the endless cycle of seasons. Twelve candles stand for months of the year. The display can be dismantled for storage.

NEED

7" wooden disc, ¼" thick

10" wooden disc, ½" thick

Wooden dowel, ½" x 36"

Wooden dowel, 1/8" x 7"

Twelve finish nails, 1"

Power drill and drill bits, 1/8" and 1/2"

Colored sheet metal piece, 12" x 12", 30-gauge

Gold spray paint

12 assorted colored candles, 12" long

Twelve inches flexible wire, matching sheet metal color

Hammer; box cutter; awl

Sandpaper

Black felt, 12" x 12"

Glue

MAKE

Place 10" wooden disc onto felt. Trace around disc. Cut circle from felt. Set aside. Mark center of small and large discs. Use ½" drill bit to drill holes through center marks. Test fit of large dowel through holes. Sand.

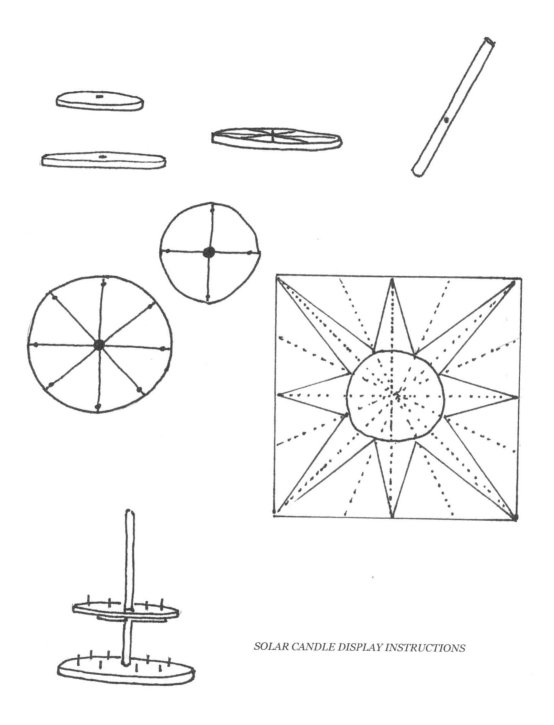

SOLAR CANDLE DISPLAY INSTRUCTIONS

Measure and mark 6" from bottom of ½" dowel. Position dowel parallel to floor and clamp dowel in vise, protecting from metal sides.

Using 1/8" drill bit, drill hole through dowel at point marked. The 1/8" dowel support piece will later be inserted through this hole.

Place 10" disc on flat surface. Use ruler and pencil to divide and mark disc into eight pie pieces. Next, measure and mark points 1/2" in from where each outside ray meets disc circumference. Hammer nail through each pencil point so nail head is flush with disc surface. Nails will hold candles onto disc.

Repeat process with 7" disc, marking disc into four pieces and hammering 4 nails through marked points, ½" in from circumference.

Spray paint both sides of two wooden discs and dowels. Allow to dry.

Center 7" wooden disc onto metal sheet and trace circle. Set aside wooden disc. Mark dot at center of metal circle. Using pencil and ruler, divide and mark circle into 16 sections, extending each line to edge of metal sheet. These will be lines for sun rays. Create sun rays by connecting alternate ray endpoints at metal sheet edge to intersections of adjacent ray/circumference.

On protected surface, use box cutter to cut outline of sun and rays. Pass over metal lightly 2-3 times versus one hard pass. Puncture small hole in sun center.

Feed wire through hole at sun center and attach to dowel, near top.

Glue felt onto smooth side of 10" disc. Allow to dry.

To assemble Solar Candle Display, carefully pierce each candle base with nail protruding from disc. With assistance, hold large dowel vertically, sun at top. Position dowel over hole in 7" disc, then carefully raise disc with candles along dowel to just above drilled hole. Feed smaller dowel through hole. Lower 7" disc over smaller dowel support. Next, position end of dowel into hole in middle of 10" disc. Spread greenery around outside of the bottom disc. Light candles.

Sun Mobile

NEED

Plywood, 12"x12"; Power jigsaw; power drill, 1/16" drill bit

Gold spray paint, twelve round tree ornaments, various colors

Clear plastic thread or gold thread, thirteen 1/4" beads, gold or black

MAKE

Draw 8" diameter circle on plywood middle. Find and mark circle center. Using pencil and ruler, divide circle in half, then quarters, extending radius lines two inches beyond circle border. Divide each quarter into thirds, until circle has 12 pie pieces. Extend each line two inches beyond outside of circle circumference.

Draw 10" circle outside 8" circle on plywood. Connect alternate ray endpoints to intersections of adjacent ray/circumference to meet at 10" perimeter. Continue around circle until there are twelve rays. Draw a 7 1/2" circle inside 8" circle.

At every indentation of a ray along 7 1/2" circle, drill a small hole, large enough to feed thread through. There will be twelve holes in all. Drill an additional hole through dot at middle of circle.

With jigsaw, remove excess outside wood, revealing sun ray shapes.

Spray or hand paint both disc sides. Allow to dry.

Cut 12" thread. Attach bead to one end. Feed other end of thread through hole in sun center. Form loop at end for hanging mobile when completed.Cut additional thread into six 6" pieces. Tie one bead onto one end piece. Thread opposite end through alternate holes in disc top.

Cut six 8" thread pieces. Tie one bead onto each 8" end piece. Thread opposite end through alternate holes in disc top. Tie ornaments onto hanging ends. Hang mobile, adjusting ornament strings to balance display.

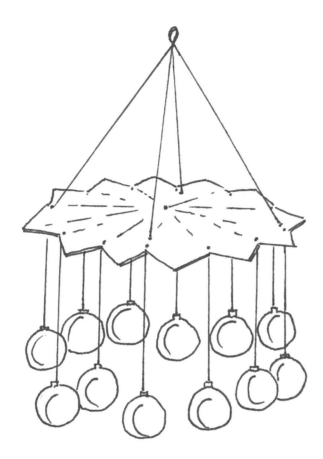

SUN MOBILE

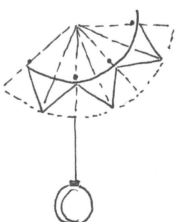

Fir Cone Garland

NEED

25 evergreen cones, various sizes

Hot glue gun and glue

Clear polyurethane spray

Red satin ribbon, 1"x36"

Flexible wire

Newspaper

MAKE

Arrange evergreen cones onto newspaper in pleasing cascade shape, using variety of shapes and sizes.

Connect large evergreen cones together with wire.

On garland back, form and fasten wire loop for hanging.

Use glue gun to affix smaller evergreen cones between large cones.

Allow garland to rest for one hour.

Spray display with polyurethane spray. Allow to dry.

Form ribbon into bow, leaving ends flowing. Use flexible wire to fasten ribbon to garland.

Calendar

There is interesting history and meaning behind the names of months. Add this information to a blank calendar template.

JANUARY—after Janus, Roman god of gates and doors, beginnings and endings.

FEBRUARY—month of expiation. Roman festival of purification was February 15. Last month of Roman calendar. After 450 BCE, February became second month. February's Old English name was Solmonath, "mud month."

MARCH—after Mars, god of war. First month in ancient Roman calendar. Began at Vernal Equinox.

APRIL—means latter or second because it came after March, the first month in ancient Rome. Derived from Latin word, "aperine," "to open," or Etruscan word related to Aphrodite, goddess of love and beauty.

MAY—after Maia, earth goddess of increase.

JUNE—after Juno, queen of gods and goddess of marriage, sister and wife of Jupiter.

JULY—named by Mark Antony to honor Julius Caesar. Pronounced "Julie" or "July" with accent on first syllable. Formerly known as Quintilis, "the fifth month."

AUGUST—after Augustus Caesar, first Roman emperor. Earlier Old English name was Weodmonath, "month of weeds."

SEPTEMBER—seventh month when year began in March.

OCTOBER—eighth month when year began in March.

NOVEMBER—ninth month when year began in March.

DECEMBER—tenth month when year began in March. Earlier Old English name was Blotmonath, "month of sacrifice." Because early Saxons were butchering at this time, animals were offered as sacrifice.

Wheel of the Year Wreath

A wreath symbolizes the wheel of the year as seasons complete their cycle. "Yule" in Old Saxon means "wheel."

NEED

Grapevine wreath

Assorted appropriately sized items from nature to represent each season

Thread, glue, or other product used to attach items to wreath

Ribbon, ¼" x 18"—white, green, pastel, vibrant, muted earth tones

MAKE

Suggestions for nature collection:

Winter—stick and holy bundles

Spring—feathers, tiny bird's nest, eggshell

Summer—vial of ocean sand, dried flowers

Autumn—tiny Indian corn cobs, acorns, preserved leaves

Attach winter items to upper quarter of wreath. Attach spring items to adjacent quarter. Attach summer items to bottom quarter. Attach autumn items to remaining quarter. Weave in ribbon to correspond to quadrant's season.

WHEEL OF THE YEAR WREATH

FOOD

Whether using new or old recipes, foods representative of the season are a joy to create and consume.

Celtic Cross Bread

The Sun Symbol, or Celtic Cross, is believed to have originated around 3000 BCE in the Western Carpathian region, far from the British Isles. It appeared first on pottery, then later on works of metal during the Beaker culture. Often found on gold objects, experts believe it was a symbol for the sun. Its use spread across Europe and the British Isles. Irish people used it so frequently, it became known as a mark of their work.

NEED

6 1/4 cups flour

1 package active dry yeast

2 1/4 cups milk

2 tablespoons sugar

1 tablespoon canola oil

1 egg, beaten

MAKE

Heat milk, sugar, and oil , then cool until lukewarm.

In a large bowl, combine 2 1/2 cups flour with yeast. Add milk mixture. Beat on low speed for 30 seconds, then high for 3 minutes. With large wooden spoon, gradually combine remaining flour. Knead dough 10 minutes.

Oil mixing bowl and drop kneaded dough into it. Turn dough over several times to distribute oil. Cover with clean cloth and let rise 90 minutes, or until doubled.

Punch down dough. Divide in half. Set aside one half.

Divide first half into three parts, one two times larger than the others. Form large piece into a ring. Roll two smaller pieces into snake shapes long enough to form a Celtic Cross over the empty ring center.

Place bread on greased or parchment paper covered cookie sheet. Repeat with remaining dough. Cover both with clean cloth and let rise 45 minutes.

Preheat oven to 375 degrees.

Brush top of dough with beaten egg.

Bake 45 minutes or until golden. If browning occurs before inside is cooked, cover top loosely with foil. Makes 2 loaves.

Seasons Bread

This artful circular loaf is a reminder that all seasons have a place in the year.

NEED

Use recipe for Celtic Cross Bread.

MAKE

Following Celtic Cross Bread recipe, roll dough into disc shape prior to last rising.

Before baking, slice deep cuts into surface to create four quarters. Into first section, carve summer motif; into the next, a fall motif; next winter motif; next spring motif.

Brush top and sides with beaten egg mixed with ½ teaspoon water.

Bake 35-45 minutes, or until golden.

SEASONS BREAD

Gingerbread Window Cookies

The Pennsylvania Dutch often hung cookies in windows during the Christmas season. Cookie shapes such as roosters (fertility), goblins (spirits), and animals (sacrifice), are reminders of ancient Teutonic symbols and rituals. Trace stencil designs onto heavy cardboard. Cut. Laminate if desired.

NEED

6 tablespoons butter, softened

3/4 cup brown sugar, packed

1 large egg

1/2 cup molasses

2 teaspoons vanilla

3 cups flour

1 1/2 teaspoons baking powder

3/4 teaspoons baking soda

1 tablespoon ginger

1 3/4 teaspoon cinnamon

1/4 teaspoon cloves

Red or Green ribbon, for hanging

MAKE

Cream butter and sugar. Add egg and beat well. Add molasses and vanilla. Beat until smooth.

In separate bowl, combine flour, baking powder, baking soda, ginger, cinnamon and cloves. Gradually add to butter/molasses mixture. Mix until blended. Divide dough in half. Wrap in wax paper. Refrigerate for several hours.

Preheat oven to 375 degrees.

Remove one dough package from refrigerator. Divide in half. On floured surface, roll out ¼" thick. Position flour-dusted stencils onto dough. Cut around shapes. Transfer cookie shapes to greased or parchment paper covered cookie sheet. Repeat with remaining dough.

Bake cookies for 7-10 minutes; longer if cookies are large. At 5 minute marker, rotate pans to encourage even browning.

Remove from oven. Immediately use toothpick to form a hole in cookie to thread ribbon later. Allow cookies to cool briefly on tray. Transfer to cookie rack to cool completely. Thread ribbon through hole. Hang cookies in windows.

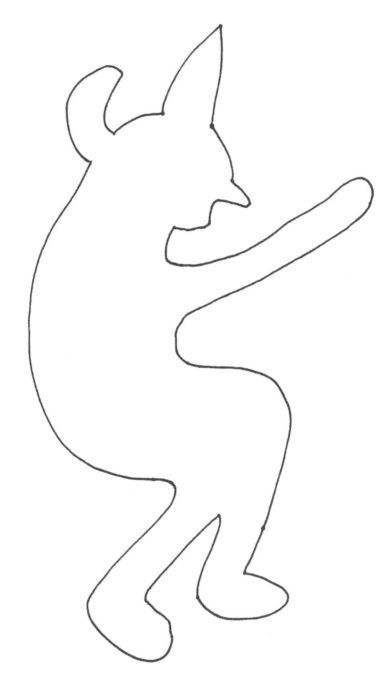

GINGERBREAD WINDOW COOKIE STENCIL

GINGERBREAD WINDOW COOKIE STENCIL

Sacrificial Cookies

Druids placed candles on tree branches to honor the god Balder. They hung apples from branches of oak and fir trees to honor the god Woden. Offerings of special cakes were baked in shapes of fish, birds, and other common animals.

These cookie shapes are reminiscent of those practices. Trace stencil designs onto heavy cardboard. Cut. Laminate if desired.

NEED

1 cup butter, softened

1 cup sugar

3 eggs

1 tablespoon vanilla

1 teaspoon ground mace

4 cups flour

MAKE

Cream butter and sugar. Add eggs and vanilla. Beat well.

In separate bowl, measure 1 cup flour. Add mace. Combine flour/mace to butter mixture and beat well. Gradually add remaining 3 cups flour. Mix until blended.

Divide dough into two parts. Wrap separately in wax paper. Chill for 2 hours.

Preheat oven to 375 degrees.

On floured surface, roll dough out to 1/8" thickness. Position flour-dusted stencils onto dough and cut around shapes. Transfer cookie shapes to greased or parchment covered cookie sheet. Repeat with remaining dough.

Bake 7-10 minutes. Cool on cookie rack.

Makes 20 large or 40 small cookies.

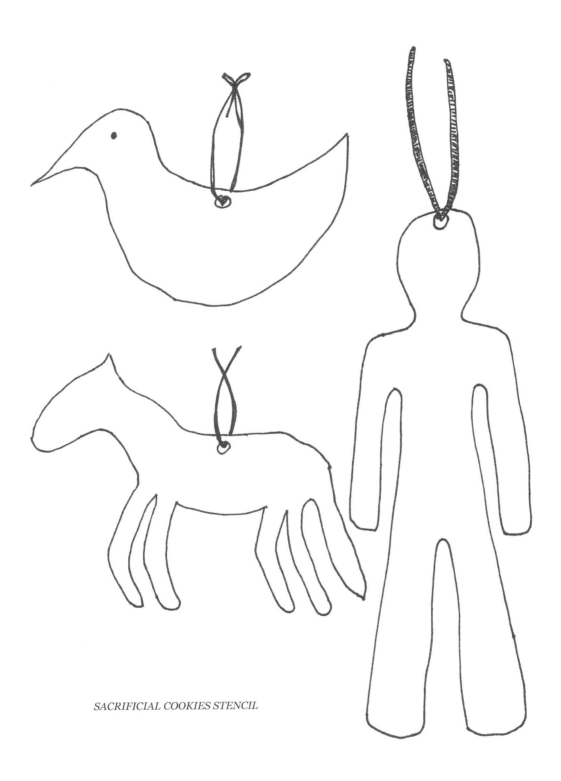

SACRIFICIAL COOKIES STENCIL

Springerle

This traditional German cookie ("little horse") has ancient pagan roots. Germanic tribes celebrated Julefest by sacrificing animals. Cut cookie shapes with a special springerle roller, or use tiny animal cookie cutters or cardboard stencils.

NEED

4 eggs

2 cups sugar

Rind from 2 lemons, grated

3 cups flour

1 teaspoon baking powder

¼ cup whole anise seeds

MAKE

In large bowl, beat eggs until light. Add sugar incrementally. Beat until pale and thick. Add grated lemon rind.

In separate bowl, combine flour and baking powder.

Add flour mixture to egg mixture and beat until dough is smooth. Add up to ½ cup additional flour, if needed. Wrap dough in wax paper. Chill 1 hour.

On floured surface, roll dough 1/3" thick.

Sprinkle with anise seeds.

Use springerle roller, cookie cutter, or flour-dusted stencil, to cut shapes.

Transfer to parchment paper covered cookie sheet. Allow to rest 24 hours.

Preheat oven to 325 degrees. Bake for 15-20 minutes. Do not brown.

Cool. Store 10 days in airtight container before consuming.

SPRINGERLE STENCIL

Mincemeat

Christmas Pie, also known as mince pie, shred pie, or mutton pie, was a popular dessert in England. The first pies were made with minced partridges, pheasants and hares, or other birds and animals. In later years, chopped meat, suet, sugar, apples, molasses, cider, raisins, currants, citron, cloves and nutmeg were added. These pies could be very large. Sometimes the meat alone in the pie weighed six pounds.

Pies were always given to visitors during holidays. Eating one pie would give one month of good luck. Twelve months of good fortune would occur in the year if one ate bites from twelve pies in twelve different places between Christmas and Twelfth Night.

Mincemeat cookies

NEED

3 eggs

1/2 teaspoon vanilla

1 1/2 cups sugar

1 cups shortening

3 1/4 cups flour

1 teaspoon baking soda

1 cup chopped walnuts

1 1/2 cups mincemeat

MAKE

Preheat oven to 350 degrees.

Cream eggs, vanilla, sugar, and shortening.

In separate bowl, combine flour and baking soda.

Add shortening mixture. Beat well.

Add nuts and mincemeat. Mix until blended.

Grease or cover a cookie sheet with parchment paper.

Using a teaspoon and knife, drop ball-shaped dough onto cookie sheet.

Bake for 10-12 minutes.

Cookies will be moist.

Cool on rack.

Makes 3 dozen.

WASSAIL

Wassail

Waesheil! Be Well! Drinc-Heil! Drink Well! Sharing a toast and a drink from the Wassail Bowl was an important pledge between friends. A pagan farmer custom was to wassail fruit trees. He would sprinkle them with cider, pour cider on the roots, hit the trunk with sticks, then chant to the tree to encourage fertility. Large pails of cider with toast floating on top were also taken out to orchards where wassailers surrounded the healthiest trees. This custom was passed down from ancient times when both cider and toast were offered to the spirit of vegetation guarding the tree.

To add ceremony to the Wassail, place the bowl on the center of a round table and distribute silver spoons to all attending. Guests walk clockwise around the table, stirring the Wassail with their right hands. As they walk and stir, every other person passes under the arm of the person preceding them.

NEED

4 small apples, 1 medium orange

1 cup sugar

13 whole cloves

2 quarts hard apple cider

½ cup brandy

1 tablespoon powdered ginger

1 teaspoon grated nutmeg

6 allspice berries

2 cinnamon sticks

6 large eggs, separated

Cheesecloth

Tiny toast triangles, optional

MAKE

Preheat oven to 350 degrees.

Core apples. Fill each cavity with 1 tablespoon sugar. Place in baking dish.

Stud orange with cloves and place in dish with apples.

Bake 40 minutes.

Place allspice berries and cinnamon sticks into cheesecloth. Tie ends securely, forming a sachet. Set aside.

Beat egg yolks until light colored. Set aside.

Beat egg whites until stiff. Set aside.

Pour cider and brandy into stock pot. Warm over moderate heat.

Whisk ginger and nutmeg into warmed liquid. Add sachet. Keep liquid warm. Do not boil.

Remove 1 cup warmed liquid from stock pot. Add liquid gradually to egg yolks, to temper.

Remove spice sachet from stock pot.

Add tempered egg yolks to stock pot.

Fold egg whites into stock pot.

Transfer to punch/wassail bowl.

Float baked apples and orange in wassail bowl.

Top individual serving with toast triangle.

Lamb's Wool

During the Middle Ages, a variety of concoctions filled the Wassail Bowl. Ingredients reflected the affluence of the owner. "Lamb's Wool" traditionally filled silver bowls of rich English families. Made of roasted crab apples, beaten eggs, sugar, and spices mixed into hot ale, the name comes from the smooth and soft texture of apples floating on top. Pieces of bread called toast were floated on top of the Wassail. When a toast was scooped up and swallowed, good wishes were declared to surrounding guests; hence, drinking a "toast." After the bowl was filled with as much as ten gallons of Lamb's Wool, it was carried by villagers from door to door so they could toast each other. In England, poor people would travel among houses of the rich to beg in rhyme for a cup of Lamb's Wool.

Legend says that a beautiful Saxon maiden named Rowena brought Prince Vortigen a bowl of wine and said "Waes Haeil" as she served him; thus starting the tradition.

Lamb's Wool is unusual and foreign to the modern palate but is included here for history's sake.

1633 Lamb's Wool Recipe

Boil three pints of ale, beat six eggs the whites and yolks together, set both on the fire in a pewter pot; add roasted apples, sugar, blanched almonds or beaten nutmeg; add cast on cinnamon, cloves and ginger; and being well brewed, drink it while hot.

Modern Lamb's Wool Recipe

NEED

6 cooking apples, peeled and sliced in ½" thick crescents

3 pints ale

6 egg whites, beaten stiff

3-6 tablespoons sugar

1/2 teaspoon ground ginger

1/2 teaspoon grated nutmeg

½ teaspoon cinnamon

Place apples on parchment paper covered cookie sheet. Bake in 250 degree oven until apples are moist and soft, approximately 15 minutes.

Gently heat ale.

Place apples into large bowl.

Pour hot ale over apples. Add sugar and spices. Leave in warm place 30 minutes.

Fold in egg whites.

Gently reheat. Serve hot.

Hot Buttered Cider

Hard cider contains alcohol. It was used to toast fruit trees and make merry.

NEED

7 cups apple cider

2 apples, sliced paper thin

1/3 cup brown sugar

1 cinnamon stick

1 teaspoon whole allspice

1 teaspoon whole cloves

Peel from 1 lemon, cut into strips

1 cup rum

Butter

Cheesecloth

MAKE

Combine spices with lemon peel. Secure in cheesecloth, forming sachet.

Pour cider into stockpot. Add brown sugar, cinnamon stick, and spice sachet.

Bring cider to boil, then reduce heat. Simmer 15 minutes.

Remove spice bag and cinnamon stick.

Add rum. Stir well.

Pour cider into individual mugs. Top with apple slice and thin pat of butter.

Serves 6-8

Glögg

There are numerous versions of this Swedish drink. A traditional recipe requires the Swedish liquor aquavit to be poured over a silver dish of sugar, then set alight. Warmed ingredients are then added to extinguish the flame. It is stirred before serving. Glögg comes from the Swedish words "to burn" or "glow." Aquavit is a Scandinavian spirit distilled from grain or potatoes. It means "water of life."

NEED

1 bottle dry red wine

1/2 cup raisins

1/2 cup aquavit (or vodka or brandy)

1/3 cup sugar

Peel from one orange

2 sticks cinnamon, 6 whole cloves, 2 cardamom pods, opened

1/2 cup whole almonds, blanched

Cheesecloth

MAKE

Blanch almonds by dropping into pot of boiling water for 1 minute. Drain and set aside.

In a stockpot, combine wine, raisins, aquavit, and sugar.

Place orange peel, cloves, and cardamom onto cheesecloth square, creating sachet.

Add spice sachet and cinnamon to wine.

Simmer wine mixture 10 -15 minutes until very hot but not boiling.

Pour glögg into individual mugs. Add a few almonds to each mug. Serves 6

Food

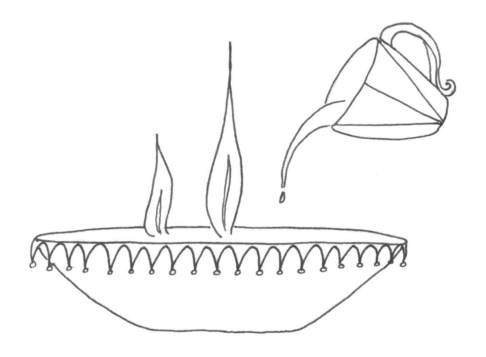

GLÖGG

227

Whipcol

A Yule breakfast in Shetland, England called for the use of a salver—a large china punch bowl complete with glasses twisted into strange shapes. The collection was only used for this occasion. It was filled with whipcol, a Yule breakfast drink of unknown origin, possibly introduced by Vikings.

NEED

12 fresh eggs*

2 ¼ cups sugar

1 cup rum

3 cups cream

MAKE

In large bowl, whip cream until stiff. Set aside.

In separate large bowl, whip eggs and sugar until light yellow.

Stir in rum.

Fold in whipped cream.

Serve immediately.

*Use caution when consuming raw eggs.

Ale Posset

The last thing drunk on Christmas Eve in Britain was an ale posset. Each family member would sip from this mixture of beer and milk. In order to enjoy good health during the coming new year, it was customary to eat an apple, often in a piece of apple pie.

NEED

6 beaten eggs

1/2 cup sugar

1/2 teaspoon freshly ground nutmeg

3 cups milk

1 cup ale, dry sherry, or hard cider

MAKE

In stockpot, combine eggs, sugar, and nutmeg.

Gradually add milk.

Cook over low heat, stirring constantly to prevent boiling.

When thickened, remove from heat.

Carefully stir in ale, sherry, or cider.

Serve hot, or chill and serve cold.

8-10 servings

Rispudding (Norwegian Rice Pudding)

In Denmark, rice pudding is a first course item at Christmas Eve dinner. A single almond is stirred into the pot before the pudding is served. The lucky almond recipient is granted one wish from other guests and treated as royalty for the evening. Other traditions claim whoever receives the nut will be next to marry, or, if already married, will have similar good fortune. Another variation is that whoever eats the most pudding will live longest.

A bowl of rice pudding placed outside farmyard or garden placates ancient little gnome-like men called Nisser. These bearded and twisted gnomes dress in red and wear smocks and tiny clogs. Some stories about Nisser are over 4000 years old. They are portrayed as spirits of ancestors who control family destiny and finances. Contemporary Nisser have been sanitized and softened to appeal to a more commercialized population.

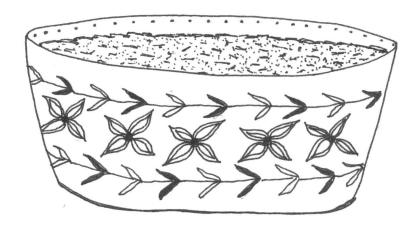

This slow cooking recipe is perfect for a snowy day of bread or cookie baking.

NEED

1/2 cup uncooked white rice

4 cups milk

3 tablespoons sugar

MAKE

In heavy saucepan, combine 1 cup milk with rice and sugar.

Cook rice over very low heat. Stir frequently.

Add additional cup of milk after first cup has been absorbed. Continue frequent stirring. Keep heat low. Do not allow milk to boil.

Add remaining milk in one cup increments, insuring each cup is absorbed before adding another. This process will take approximately 2 hours.

Serve pudding warm or cold. Add a few raisins. Sprinkle cinnamon and sugar over each serving.

Saint Lucia Rolls

Serve these warm on Winter Solstice Morning.

NEED

3/4 cup milk

1/2 teaspoon saffron threads

1/4 cup sugar

One packet active dry yeast

4 cups flour

1/2 teaspoon salt

1/4 cup butter, softened

1/4 cup sour cream

2 eggs

Raisins, 2 per roll

MAKE

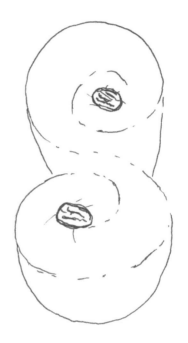

In a small pot, combine saffron and milk. Heat gently.

Cool milk to lukewarm. Add yeast. Stir to dissolve. Let stand 10 minutes, until frothy.

In mixing bowl, combine flour, sugar, and salt. Add milk mixture, 1 egg, butter, sour cream. Using mixer dough hook, knead dough 4-5 minutes.

Cover bowl. Allow dough to rise in draft-free place, 2 hours, or until doubled.

Punch down dough. Knead for 1 minute. Divide dough in half, quarters, eighths, etc., to create shapes slightly larger than golf-balls.

Roll balls into 8-10 inch snakes. Connect ends, creating oval ropes. Twist ropes in middle to create figure eight shapes. Place on parchment covered cooking tray. Or, shape snakes into "S" shapes, scrolling ends.

Cover tray and let rolls rise in draft-free place 1 hour, or until doubled.

Push raisin in side centers of figure eight circles, or inside scrolls of "S" shapes.

In small dish, mix egg with 1 teaspoon water. Brush onto rolls.

Bake in 400 degree oven, 10 minutes. Makes 2 dozen large rolls.

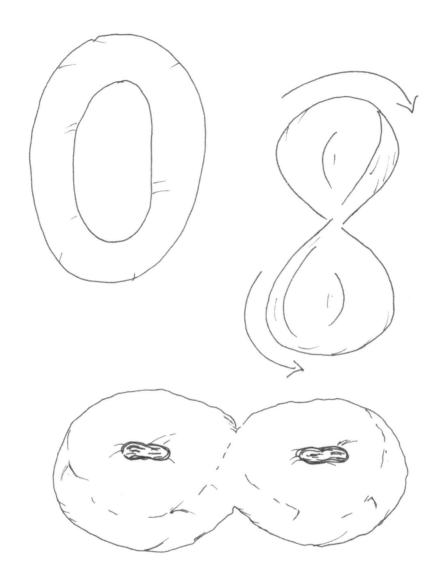

LEAF COOKIES STENCIL

Leaf Cookies

The Druids worshipped trees. The oak tree was most revered but others, including the pine, were also sacred.

NEED

1 1/3 cup shortening

1 1/2 cup sugar

2 teaspoons vanilla

2 eggs

3 tablespoons milk

4 cups flour

3 teaspoons baking powder

MAKE

In mixing bowl, cream shortening, sugar and vanilla.

Add egg and milk. Beat well.

In separate bowl, combine flour and baking powder. Add to wet ingredients. Mix until blended.

Divide dough into quarters. Wrap separately in wax paper. Refrigerate 1 hour.

Preheat oven to 375 degrees.

On floured surface, roll dough 1/8" thick.

Dust leaf stencils with flour, then place on dough and cut around shapes with knife.

Bake on parchment paper covered cookie tray 6-10 minutes.

Let cool slightly on pan, then transfer to cookie rack. Frost with Butter Frosting.

Makes 3-4 dozen cookies.

Butter Frosting

NEED

6 tablespoons butter

1 one pound package powdered sugar

1/4 cup milk

1 1/2 teaspoon vanilla

MAKE

Cream butter.

Gradually add half sugar until well blended. Beat in half milk and all vanilla.

Add remaining flour and enough of milk to create a spreadable consistency.

Divide frosting among 4 small containers.

Use food coloring to create yellow, red, orange, and purple frosting.

Frost cookies.

To quick-set frosting on cookie, briefly place frosted cookie in freezer.

Acorn Cookies

Greeks believed the oak was the first of all trees and the first mother. Romans agreed. According to Virgil, the human race sprung from oak:

"Of nymphs and fauns, and savage men, who took

Their birth from trunks of trees and stubborn Oak."

Use Leaf Cookie recipe to make cookie base. and cardboard stencil to shape. Color Butter Frosting tan and dark brown, or melt caramel and chocolate, then apply to cookies using craft paintbrush.

LEAF COOKIES STENCIL

Pecan Acorn Cookies

NEED

1 cup butter, softened

3/4 cup brown sugar, packed

1 ¾ cup pecans, finely chopped

1 teaspoon vanilla

2 ¾ cups flour

½ teaspoon baking powder

1 cup semisweet chocolate pieces

MAKE

Preheat oven to 325 degrees.

In large bowl, combine butter and brown sugar. Add vanilla. Mix well.

Add ¾ cup chopped pecans. Mix well.

In separate bowl, combine flour and baking powder.

Add flour mixture to mixing bowl and beat until blended.

Prepare parchment paper covered cookie sheet.

Form dough into 1" diameter balls. Place evenly on cookie sheet.

Bake 12–15 minutes. Cool on wire racks.

Melt chocolate over low heat or double boiler, stirring constantly to prevent burning.

Place remaining chopped pecans in small dish.

Dip rounded bottom of cookie into chocolate, then into chopped pecans. Cool on wax paper.

Oxen Horn Rolls

A tradition of baking Christmas loaves or pastries in shapes of animals or animal horns was popular in many parts of Europe. In Sweden and Denmark, a "Yule Boar" loaf was baked in the shape of a wild boar and stood at the table for all to enjoy throughout the Yule season. Often made from the last corn of the harvest, it was kept until sowing time when it was mixed with regular feed and then fed to plough horses and oxen to promote a good harvest. Wild boar was a popular Christmas feast item because the boar dug its tusks into the ground with an action similar to ploughing.

In France, Christmas cakes were made in horn shapes and given to the poor.

NEED

Pizza dough, homemade or purchased

1 egg yolk, beaten

MAKE

Preheat oven to 400 degrees.

Divide dough into small balls. Roll into 4" snake shapes.

On parchment covered cookie sheet, form "C" shape pairs, opposite sides together.

Add 1 teaspoon water to egg yolk. Mix. Brush rolls with egg yolk.

Bake 12 minutes.

Southern Slav Chesnitza or Kolatch Cakes

Southern Slavs baked chesnitza and kolatch cakes early on Christmas morning. These were shaped like flat wheels. Lines led away from the center hole where a small lighted candle or tiny decorated Christmas tree was placed. The head of household broke a cake with great solemnity, offering a piece to each member.

Bread and cakes baked on Christmas morning were thought to have special qualities. After the remains became dry, they were pounded into powder. Combined with hot water, they were used to ease summer illness.

NEED

1 cup warm water

1 package active dry yeast

3 ½ cups flour

1 teaspoon salt

1 tablespoon vegetable shortening

1 egg yolk, beaten

1 small coin, sanitized

Make:

Combine yeast and warm water. Set aside.

Mix egg yolk with 1 teaspoon water.

In large bowl, combine 3 cups of flour and salt. Add yeast and water. Mix until dough is no longer sticky, adding additional ½ cup flour if needed. Transfer dough to greased bowl, turn to coat with oil, then cover and let rise until doubled.

Punch dough down, cover, and let rise again.

Heat oven to 350 degrees.

Turn dough out onto lightly floured surface. Knead until shiny.

Form dough into flat round shape. Place on parchment paper covered cookie sheet. Let rise again.

Using bottom of small drinking glass, press deep into circle center. With sharp knife, create four slits, radiating from center circle. Inside each quadrant, embellish with designs resembling wheat, oats, and rye. Lightly brush designs with egg yolk.

Bake 35 minutes. Cool on wire rack.

Sun Shaped Shortbread

NEED

¾ pound butter

1 cup sugar

1 teaspoon vanilla

3 ½ cups flour

MAKE

Preheat oven to 325 degrees.

Using electric mixer, cream butter until light and fluffy.

Add sugar and vanilla. Beat until well combined.

Add flour incrementally, beating only until combined.

On parchment lined cookie tray, roll or pat dough into disc shape, ½" thick.

Use a dinner plate or bowl at least 2" smaller than dough disc to imprint a circle shape on dough.

With a knife or pizza cutter, shape sun rays into dough area outside disc. Remove excess.

Divide and shape excess dough into sun's eyebrows, eyes, nose, and lips. Place onto dough disc.

Bake for 20-40 minutes.

Cool completely. Transfer to serving platter.

SUN SHAPED SHORTBREAD

Welsh Plum Pudding

Some historians believe that plum pudding, or plum pottage, is a relative of frumenty, a dish made of boiled grains, broth, eggs or milk. Eventually, this ingredient list expanded to include sugar, lemons, raisins, currants, nutmeg, suet, ginger, mace, and cloves. It was originally served as a meat side dish during the first part of the Christmas feast.

Plum pudding grew sweeter and stiffer in consistency, and was eventually served as a dessert. In recipes for plum pudding, plums are conspicuously absent because plum means to rise or swell. In this dish, the name refers to the way raisins plump during cooking.

The origin of the first plum pudding is unknown but the English have an interesting theory. An English king hunting in the forest was forced to remain there on Christmas Eve. He combined all available food into one pot, including chopped meat, flour, apples, eggs, ale, dried plums, sugar and brandy. Mixing everything, he put it into a bag, then boiled it until it became the first plum pudding.

Every household member should participate in the preparation of plum pudding. A common custom is to place a thimble, ring, coin, or button into the pudding to positively affect the recipient's destiny.

Sprinkle pudding with sugar, and serve in a shallow puddle of flaming spirits.

Use an authentic plum pudding steamer to create a beautiful shape.

WELSH PLUM PUDDING

Plum Pudding and Hard Sauce

(William Benjamin Evans II Recipe)

NEED

1 cup currants

2 cups raisins

1 cup brown sugar

1 ½ cup coarse bread crumbs

¼ pound chopped suet, or ½ cup grated frozen butter

2 eggs, well beaten

¾ teaspoon cinnamon

¾ teaspoon nutmeg

3/8 teaspoon allspice

¼ cloves

¼ cup white wine

¼ cup brandy

1/3 cup fine cut citron

1/3 cup candied orange peel

MAKE

Combine all ingredients. Mix well.

Butter inside of pudding mold.

Pack pudding into mold. Cover securely.

Place mold into stockpot.

Fill with enough water to cover ¾ of mold.

Bring water to boil.

Cover stockpot.

Boil pudding for 6 hours, adding more heated water as needed to maintain ¾ level in stockpot.

If prepared in advance, boil additional 2 hours before serving.

Unmold and sprinkle with brandy.

Flambé.

Serves 12

Hard Sauce

NEED

½ cup butter

¾ cup powdered sugar

¼ teaspoon vanilla

1/8 teaspoon almond extract

Pinch nutmeg

MAKE

Cream butter in electric mixer.

Add sugar and mix well.

Add vanilla and almond extract.

Place sauce into small decorative dish.

Dust with cinnamon.

Place one small dollop onto each serving.

CHOCOLATE YULE LOG

Chocolate Yule Log

(Virginia Ann Blersch Evans Recipe)

Oak, once sacred and prolific in the great forests of England, was the traditional wood used for a Yule log for both Celts and Europeans. Church influence eventually exchanged oak for ash with the rationale that this was wood available to shepherds on short notice as they washed the baby Jesus. Ash is the only green wood that will burn without sputtering. Peasants continued their Yule log tradition using different wood, honoring Jesus and his birth instead of the power of nature.

NEED

5 eggs, separated

1/2 teaspoon cream of tarter

1 cup sugar

1/4 cup flour

3 tablespoons cocoa

1 teaspoon vanilla

1/4 cup powdered sugar

1 cup whipping cream for filling

MAKE

Preheat oven 325 degrees.

Cut wax paper large enough to line bottom and sides of 15" x 10" x 1" jelly-roll pan. Grease lightly. Set aside.

In small bowl, combine egg whites with cream of tartar. Beat until stiff. Gradually add ½ cup sugar.

In a separate bowl, beat egg yolks until thick and yellow.

Combine cocoa and 1/2 cup sugar. Blend into egg yolks. Add vanilla.

Gently fold egg whites into yolk mixture.

Transfer batter onto pan, spreading evenly.

Bake 25 minutes.

Cool in pan 5 minutes.

Turn cake onto dish towel sprinkled with powdered sugar.

Peel away wax paper. Cool cake to lukewarm. Trim crusts.

Roll cake in towel. Cool completely.

Whip cream until firm.

Unroll cake. Spread cream filling over surface. Roll again.

Glossy Frosting

NEED

1/2 cup sugar

1 ½ tablespoons cornstarch

1 ounce square unsweetened chocolate

1/2 cup boiling water

1 1/2 tablespoons butter

1/2 teaspoon vanilla

MAKE

In small pot, combine sugar, cornstarch, chocolate and hot water. Cook slowly until thickened.

Remove from heat. Add butter and vanilla.

Immediately frost Yule Log.

Twelfth Night Cake

England, France, Holland, Germany and Italy all enjoyed the custom of hiding a bean inside a cake, then dividing the cake among family members. The bean recipient became king or queen for the day, was granted a special chair to sit in, and enjoyed other regal treatment.

Beans have sacred status in antiquity. The philosopher/mathematician Pythagoras revered them. Pythagoras was running away from enemies when he arrived at a field of beans. He would not allow himself to go any farther because if he did, he would have to run through the field, trampling the plants. As a result, his enemies captured him.

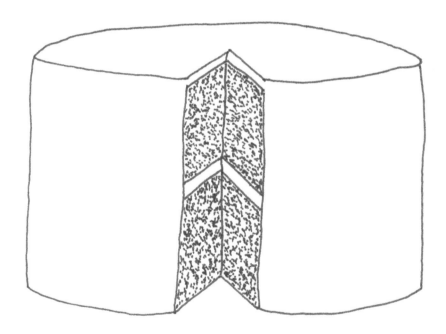

Twelfth Night by Robert Herrick

Now, now the mirth comes

With the cake full of plums

Where Beane's the King of the sport here,

Beside we must knowe

The pea also

Must revell as Quenne for the night here.

Which knowne, let us make

Joy-sops with the cake

And let not a man then be seen here,

Who inurged will not drink

To the base from the brink

A health to the King and the Queene here.

Next crowne the bowle full

With gentle lamb's wooll;

And sugar, nutmeg and ginger,

With store if ale too;

And this you must doe

To make the wassaile a stinger.

Give then to the King,

And the Queene wassailing.

And though with ale ye be whet here;

Yet part y from hence,

As free from offence,

As when ye innocent met here.

Twelfth Night Cake and Frosting

Hide a dried bean in the cooked red velvet cake before frosting.

NEED

1 cup butter, softened

2 cups granulated sugar

4 eggs

1 cup sour cream

½ cup milk

1/2 ounce red natural food coloring

2 teaspoons vanilla extract

2 ½ cups flour

½ cup unsweetened cocoa powder

1 teaspoon baking soda

MAKE

Preheat oven to 350 degrees.

Grease and flour two 9" round cake pans.

Combine butter and sugar in mixing bowl. Beat well. Add eggs. Beat well.

Add sour cream, milk, food coloring, and vanilla. Mix well.

In separate bowl, combine flour, cocoa and baking soda. Gradually add flour mixture to bowl, beating only until combined.

Pour into pans. Bake 35 minutes.

Remove from oven. Push one dried bean into top of cake. Cool, then turn onto wire rack.

Cream Cheese Frosting

NEED

8 ounces cream cheese, softened

¼ cup butter, softened

2 tablespoons sour cream

2 teaspoons vanilla extract

16 ounce box confectioners' sugar

MAKE

Spread frosting on top of first cake layer. Stack second layer onto first. Frost outsides, then top of cake.

Gingerbread Squares

Lucia queens serve cakes like these on St. Lucia Day. To create a beautiful snowy design, use a cardboard star or heart stencils. Place stencil on gingerbread square, then sift confectioner sugar over it.

NEED

½ cup butter

½ cup brown sugar

½ cup blackstrap molasses

½ boiling water

1 egg

1 ½ cup flour

½ teaspoon baking powder

½ teaspoon baking soda

1 teaspoon ginger

Confectioners sugar

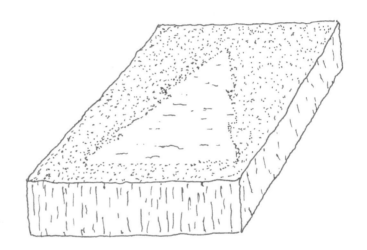

MAKE

Preheat oven to 350 degrees.

In large bowl, combine, butter, sugar, molasses, and boiling water. Mix well.

Add egg. Mix well.

In separate bowl, combine flour, baking powder, baking soda, and spices.

Combine wet and dry ingredients. Mix until blended. Pour into 9" square pan.

Bake for 35 minutes. Cut into squares. Dust with confectioners sugar designs.

Serve warm.

Pepperkaker

In Scandinavia, Yule biscuits were made and given as gifts. One biscuit was baked in a goat shape and the person who ate it was required to bleat like a goat. Crumbs from these goat biscuits were considered to have magical qualities. Many times an entire household would participate in the biscuit preparation. Twenty different types of biscuits were once made during Yule but this number has been reduced to seven.

NEED

1/2 cup sugar

1/2 cup dark corn syrup

1/2 cup butter

1 1/2 teaspoons vinegar

1 egg, beaten

2 1/4 cups flour

1/2 teaspoon baking soda

1/4 teaspoon pepper, freshly ground

1/2 teaspoon ginger

1/2 teaspoon cloves

1/2 teaspoon cinnamon

MAKE

In small pot, combine sugar, butter, vinegar, and dark corn syrup. Simmer over low heat.

Pour contents into large bowl. Cool to lukewarm. Stir in egg.

In separate bowl, combine dry ingredients. Add dry ingredients to wet ingredients. Beat until smooth.

Wrap dough into wax paper. Refrigerate several hours or overnight.

Preheat oven to 350 degrees.

Place dough on floured surface. Roll out and cut into shapes such as animals, hearts, and trees. Transfer shapes to parchment paper covered cookie tray.

Bake 7-8 minutes.

How to Make a Fire

Nothing feels more primal on a cold winter day or night than the warmth of a fire. Follow safety guidelines and enjoy.

NEED

Designated fire area located away from trees and buildings

Bucket of water, or hose with running water available

Dry leaves or dry yard matter

Assorted small dry sticks

Larger dry sticks, broken into uniform pieces

Assorted aged wood logs

Matches

MAKE

Dig small fire pit to contain fire.

In designated fire area center, place dry leaves on ground. Using small dry twigs, construct teepee shape over leaves.

Light leaves with match.

Gradually add larger sticks, taking care not to smother fire.

As fire builds, place smallest log over flaming teepee. Allow to catch fire.

Being conscious of scarves or hair, blow on fire to direct flames to log as needed.

Continue to build fire by adding logs as each log is completely engulfed by flames.

Always extinguish fire before leaving area. Pour water over embers. Stir. Add additional water.

More

Here are some shortcuts to quickly make a variety of crafts.

Thyrsus

From the Greek festival of Dionysus, symbolizes fertility, life, and revivification. Make a wand with a branch, top it with a pine cone, and attach ribbon streamers. Hang over doorway or carry in procession.

Sigillaria

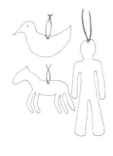

Little clay dolls exchanged in (Roman) Saturnalia festival. This custom was a forerunner of modern greeting cards. Human and animal figurines are believed to be derivative of ancient sacrificial practices. Use self-drying clay to fashion figures, poke a hole in top, thread ribbon through and hang as ornament.

Small Bundles of Wheat Sheaves

Once used to placate evil spirits believed to rush through the lone, dark nights of early winter in the lands of Norway, Sweden, and Denmark. Also used to feed birds when placed outside. Gather small bundles of dried grasses, then tie with colored ribbon

Mini Yule Logs

This custom relates to the sacred oak and Yule log of Eastern Europe. Use small branch segments as logs. Gather together with gold ribbon or wire, then embellish with red satin ribbon, leaves, and flowers. Hang as ornaments or window decorations.

Mummer's Headdress

Dancing celebrants wore these to hide identities because they believed magic could only be effective if anonymous. Fashion a headband with a wide ribbon or crepe paper and hang streamers all around to completely disguise the face.

Celtic Cross

This simple cross surrounded by a circle is a sun symbol that originated around 3000 BCE. Make one of clay or dough, poke a hole in the top, then thread a ribbon or string. Hang as ornament.

Holly Ornament

In ancient times, holly was hung in pagan temples to welcome elves and fairies. It was also hung in view of domestic animals to encourage their vitality. Use construction paper designs to replace holly if live plants are unavailable. Hang over dog or cat dishes.

Paper Boxes

Used to exchange money during the Roman Saturnalia. Fashion boxes with craft paper. Decorate with stars and sparkles. Enclose money or small gifts to surprise throughout the season.

Mini Wooden Pyramid

Gilt evergreen branches, apples, and nuts adorned large pyramids popular in England prior to 1840. Assemble smaller versions using wooden craft sticks or tiny branches. Decorate with colored paper.

Mini Mobile

Invite the spirt of nature inside. Soak a short twig until pliant, then twist together. Fasten with wire or thread. Attach sprigs of greenery, beads and feathers. Hang with ribbon or thread.

Suggestions for the Season

Donate food and clothing. Share with those less fortunate.

On the eve of the Solstice, gather together friends and family to sing to animals who endure the cold. Scatter food for them.

Make Winter Solstice Eve and Winter Solstice official family holidays.

Invite family members to collect evergreens, then construct a wreath. Add assorted herbs. Place the wreath on the front door of your home or on the center of your table. Mist daily. At season's end, return it to nature, or save it to burn in your summer solstice bonfire.

Center a circle of candles on a table. Place one large candle in the middle. As the sun sets, sit in darkness at the table. Have a senior family member light center candle and share a meditative comment about winter, darkness, light, and renewal. End with a blessing to the new year and give thanks to the earth. Encourage family members to light candles in turn and express gratitude for the old year as well as a hope for the new year. Join hands and sing together.

Save a branch of your Christmas tree to burn in next year's Yule bonfire.

Winter Solstice Celebrations of World Cultures
Past and Present:

India *Uttarayan* Northern journey (of the sun)

Spain *The Urn of Fate* The Urn is part of an old Roman custom. Family members record their names on paper and deposit into an urn. Slips of paper are drawn from it, two at a time. Each pair drawn will be devoted friends throughout the year.

Scandinavia *Shoes* Family members place shoes together to live in harmony during the coming year.

Japan *Touji* Arrival of winter is marked by eating pumpkin/squash to ward off sickness, and taking a citrus bath.

Persia (Babylonia) *Sacaea* The annual renewal festival is related to Chinese, Vedic and European writings about the twelve days of chaos representing the conflict between good and evil. The Sacaea was the forerunner of the Saturnalia at which societal restrictions were relaxed as the old year ended. Roles were exchanged between master and slave, and there was masquerading and mockery.

Iran *Shab-e-Yalda* Iranian families pass the night by the fire to help the sun god battle evil and darkness.

Pakistan *Chaomos/Chaumos* An ancient demigod returns during the winter solstice to gather prayers of the people, then delivers them to the supreme being named Dezao. Ritual purification baths are taken. Great festivities follow.

Tibet *Desmoche* A five day festival celebrates the dying year. Dancers dress in gruesome masquerade, then dance around a star covered pole to chase away evil spirits and prevent them from entering the new year. Feasting follows. Later, townspeople topple the pole.

Iceland *New Year's Eve* The evening is celebrated with fireworks to blow out the old year. A traditional Icelandic greeting to elves on New Year's Eve:

Let those who want to, arrive

Let those who want to, leave

Let those who want to, stay

Without harm to me or mine.

China *Dong Zhi* The Arrival of Winter. Although the Chinese calendar is lunar, there is a winter solstice observance called Dong Zhi or "Doing the Winter."

Peru *Inti Raymi* Three days of fasting preceded this most important of the four sun festivals held during the year. People assembled in the common square to wait for the sun to rise, then shouted with joy. A mirror was used start a fire to light altar flames at temples throughout the region. Flames were kindled all year.

North American Southwest *Soyal* Hopi Native Americans Hopi priests dressed in animal skins and feathered headdresses resembling the sun's rays as they ceremoniously marked the sun's return. Sacred structures called kivas included strategically placed slits in upper walls, allowing sun and moon rays to penetrate.

British Columbia *Kwakiutl* They changed names to those of ancestors at winter's start, protecting them from roaming spirits of the dead.

Afterword

Ancient paganism is occasionally and erroneously associated with the Wicca religion commonly referred to as Witchcraft. While a modern witch "calls" spirits to work with her, an ancient pagan would not have authority to summon any power to an earthly site. Pagans tried instead to appease powers.

Ancient paganism may have its own set of easily criticized practices, but ancient pagans did not practice magic. Magic is the basis for witchcraft. This modern connection between witchcraft and ancient paganism can foster further misunderstanding when applied equally to both philosophies.

This comment is not meant to criticize Wicca but rather to highlight the distinction between it and ancient paganism.

Bibliography

Adler, Margot. *Drawing Down the Moon*. Boston: Beacon, 1986.

Ancient Christmas Carols: With the Tunes to Which They Were Formerly Sung in the West of England. Collected by Davies Gilbert. London: John Nichols and Son, 1822.

Ashton, John. *A Right Merrie Christmas!!! The Story of Christ-tide*. NY: Benjamin Bloom, 1968.

Auld, William Muir. *Christmas Traditions*. NY: Macmillan, 1931.

Bede. *The Ecclesiastical History of England*.

Bellingham, David. *Goddesses, Heroes & Shamans: The Young People's Guide to World Mythology*. NY: Kingfisher, 1997.

Berens, E.M. *Myths of Ancient Greece and Rome*.

Betty Crocker's New International Cookbook. NY: Prentice Hall, 1989.

Blundell, W. *A History of the Isle of Man*. Edited by W. Harrison. Manx Society, 1859.

Braden, Charles Samuel. *The World's Religions*. NY: Abdingdon Press, 1939.

Brown, Dale. *The Cooking of Scandinavia*. NY: Time, 1968.

Bunning, Patricia Stevens. *Merry Christmas! A History of the Holiday*. Antheneum, 1979

Cabot, Laurie. *Celebrate the Earth: A Year of Holidays in the Pagan Tradition*. NY: Delta, 1994.

Cade, Sharon. *Special Days: History, Folklore, and Whatnot*. Portland, OR: SC Enterprises, 1984.

Campanelli, Pauline. *Ancient Ways: Reclaiming Pagan Traditions*. St. Paul, MN: Llewellyn, 1993.

Carey, Diana and Judy Large. *Festivals, Families and Food*. UK: Hawthorne, 1982.

Carlson, Eric. *The Holiday Wreath Book*. NY: Sterling, 1992.

Carpenter, Edward. *Pagan & Christian Creeds: Their Origins & Meanings*. NY: Harcourt, Brace & Howe, 1920.

Christmas Around the World: A Celebration. New York: Sterling Publishing, 1978.

Clancy, John. *John Clancy's Christmas Cookbook*. NY: Hearst, 1982.

Clare, John D. *The Vikings*. NY: Gulliver, 1992.

Collins, Marie and Virginia Davis. *A Medieval Book of Seasons*. NY: Harper Collins, 1992.

Commonplace Book of Richard Hill. London, 1503–1536.

Cooper, Stephanie, Christina Fynes Clinton, and Mary Rowling. *The Children's Year*. UK: Hawthorne, 1986.

Count, Earl W. and Alice Lawson Count. *4000 Years of Christmas: A Gift from the Ages.* Berkeley, CA: Ulysses, 1997.

Crichton, Robert. *Who is Santa Claus? The True Story Behind a Living Legend.* Edinburgh: Cannongate, Ltd., 1989.

Cure, Karen. *An Old Fashioned Christmas: American Holiday Traditions.* NY: Harry N. Abrams, 1984.

Del Re, Gerard and Patricia Del Re. *The Christmas Almanack.* Garden City, NY: Doubleday, 1979.

Dunkling, Leslie. *A Dictionary of Days.* NY, Facts on File, 1988.

Ebel, Holly. *Christmas In the Air: An Old Fashioned Book for an Old Fashioned Christmas.* Minneapolis: Holly Day, 1986.

Eliade, Mircea. *A History of Religious Ideas. Vol. 1. From the Stone Age to the Eleusinian Mysteries.* Translated by Willard R. Trask. Chicago: University of Chicago Press, 1978.

Ellis, Peter Berresford. The Druids. Grand Rapids, MI: William B. Eerdmans, 1995.

Evans, Cheryl. *Usborne Illustrated Guide to Norse Myths & Legends.* UK: E.D.C., 1987.

Falls, C.B. *The First 5000 Years.* NY: Viking Press.

Fitzgibbon, Theodora. *A Taste of Scotland.* NY: Avenel, 1970.

Frazer, James G. *The Golden Bough: The Roots of Religion and Folklore.* NY: Avenel, 1981.

Funk & Wagnalls. *Standard Dictionary of Folklore, Mythology, & Legend.* NY: Harper & Row, 1972

Genest, Emile. *Myths of Ancient Greece & Rome.* London: Burke, 1968.

Golby, J.M. and A.W. Purdue. *The Making of Modern Christmas.* Athens, GA: University of Georgia Press, 1986.

Gorham, Melvin. *The Pagan Bible.* Portland, OR: Binfords & Mort, 1962.

Haedrich, Ken. *Home for the Holidays: Festive Baking with Whole Grains.* NY: Bantom, 1992.

Hale, William Harlan and Editors of Horizon Magazine. *The Horizon Cookbook and Illustrated History of Eating and Drinking Through the Ages.* Rockville, MD: American Heritage, 1968.

Halliday, W.R. *The Pagan Background of Early Christianity.* NY: Cooper Square, 1970.

Harris, Geraldine. *Gods and Pharaohs from Egyptian Mythology.* British Columbia: Eurobooks, 1982.

Hayward, John. *The Encyclopedia of Ancient Civilizations of the Near East and Mediterranean.* Armonk, NY: M.E. Sharpe, 1979.

Heinberg, Richard. *Celebrate the Solstice: Honoring the Earth's Seasonal Rhythms Through Festival & Ceremony.* Wheaton, IL: Quest, 1993.

Hole, Christina. *Christmas & Its Customs.* NY: M.Barrows, 1958.

Bibliography

Holidays, Festivals, and Celebrations of the World Dictionary. Compiled by Sue Ellen Thomspson and Barbara W. Carlson. MI: Omnigraphics, 1994.

Horace J. Gardner. *Let's Celebrate Christmas.* NY: A.S. Barnes, 1950.

Hutton, Ronald. *The Pagan Religions of the Ancient British Isles: Their Nature and Legacy.* Oxford, UK: Blackwell, 1991.

Jackson, Ellen. *The Winter Solstice.* Brookfield, CT: Millbrook, 1994.

Jacqueline Ridley, ed. *Christmas Around the World: A Celebration.* NY: Sterling, 1985.

James, E. O. *Seasonal Feasts & Festivals.* NY: Barnes & Noble, 1961.

Jones, Gertrude. *The Dictionary of Mythology, Folklore and Symbols.* NY: Scarecrow, 1961.

Jones, Prudence and Nigel Pennick. *A History of Pagan Europe.* NY: Routledge, 1995.

Karas, Sheryl Ann. *The Solstice Evergreen.* Boulder Creek, CA: Ashlan, 1991.

Krythe, Maymie. *All About Christmas.* New York: Harper, 1954.

Leach, Maria, ed. *The Standard Dictionary of Folklore, Mythology and Legend.* NY: Funk and Wagnalls, 1950.

MacDonald, Margaret Read. *The Folklore of World Holidays.* Detroit: Gale Research, 1992.

Maks, Michele. *Wreathmaking from the State of Maine.* Camden, ME: Down East Books, 1987.

Matthews, Caitlin and John Matthews. *The Western Way.* London: Arkana, 1985.

Matthews, Caitlin. *The Elements of the Celtic Tradition.* UK: Element Books, 1989.

Miles, Clement and T. Fisher Unwin. *Christmas in Ritual & Tradition, Christian and Pagan.* London: Adelphi Terrace, 1912.

Muir, Frank. *Christmas Customs and Traditions.* NY: Taplinger, 1975.

Munsen, Sylvia. *Cooking the Norwegian Way.* Minneapolis: Lerner Publications, 1982.

Nichols, Ross. *The Book of Druidry: History, Sites and Wisdom.* San Francisco: Aquarian, 1975.

Nissenbaum, Stephen. *The Battle for Christmas.* NY: Alfred A. Knopf, 1996.

Paris, Ginette. *Pagan Meditations: The Worlds of Aphrodite, Artemis, and Hestia.* Dallas: Spring, 1986.

Pearson, Nora Florence. *The Stories of Our Christmans Customs.* Loughborough, UK: Ladybird, 1964.

Pennick, Nigel. *Pagan Book of Days: A Guide to the Festivals, Traditions and Sacred Days of the Year.* VT: Destiny, 2001.

Relph, Ingeborg and Penny Stanway. *Christmas: A Cook's Tour.* Batavia, IL: Lion Publishing, 1991.

Robert Chambers. *The Book of Days: A Miscellany of Popular Antiquities in Connection with the Calendar, Including Anecdote, Biography, & History, Curiosities of Literature and Oddities of Human Life and Character...* 1864.

Roberts, J.M.. *History of the World*. Oxford: Oxford University Press, 1993.

Rogers, Robert William. *A History of Ancient Persia*. NY: Charles Scribner's Sons, 1929.

Room, Adrian. *NTS's Dictionary of Word Origins*. Lincolnwood, IL: NTC, 1992.

Rose, Carol. *Spirits, Fairies, Gnomes and Goblins*. Santa Barbara, CA: ABC-CLIO, 1996.

Sarnoff, Jane and Reynold Ruffins. *Light the Candles! Beat the Drums!* NY: Scribner, 1979

Simpson, Jacqueline. *European Mythology*. NY: Peter Bedrick, 1987.

Spawforth, Antony. *The Oxford Classical Dictionary*. Oxford University Press, 1996.

Spicer, Dorothy. *46 Days of Christmas*. NY: Coward, McCann & Geoghegan, 1960.

Sterbenz, Carol Endler and Nancy Johnson. *The Decorated Tree: Recreating Traditional Christmas Ornaments*. NY: Abrams, 1982.

Streep, Peg. *Sanctuaries of the Goddess*. Boston: Bulfinch, 1994.

The Anthenaeum. Notes and Queries, 1st Series, vol. v, 5, London: 1848

The Barnhart Dictionary of Etymology. Edited by Robert K. Barnhart. NY: H.W.Wilson, 1988.

Tom Hartman, ed. *Guinness Book of Christmas*. NY: Sterling, 1984.

Toulson, Shirley. *The Winter Solstice*. N.P.: Morgan & Morgan, 1982.

Van Renterghem, Tony. *When Santa Was A Shaman*. St. Paul, MN: Llewellyn, 1995.

Wernecke, Herbert H. *Christmas Customs Around the World*. Louisville, KY: Westminster John Knox, 1979.

Wyndham, Lee. *Holidays in Scandinavia*. Champaign, IL: Garrad, 1975.

Yan, Erna Olson and Sigrid Marstrander. *Time Honored Norwegian Recipes*. Decorah, IA: Norwegian-American Museum, 1990.

Yolen, Jane. *Hark! A Christmas Sampler*. NY: G.P.Putnam's Sons, 1991.

Index